COMMUNICATING OVER TROUBLED WATERS

VARUN SHARMA

For Ruchika, my companion on this magical journey

And my parents, Pardeep and Neelam Sharma

Contents

Acknowledgements

I have spent my twenties working in training and development along with banking.

I have been inspired by many extraordinary people. There are, as they say, far too many to thank individually. Nonetheless, I do need to thank specific people who directly impacted my journey and this book.

Ruchika, my wife, was the first person to go through the manuscript. She helped me through this entire time. From writing the book from scratch to deciding on the cover of the book. And most importantly believing in me.

My parents Pardeep and Neelam Sharma for the unconditional support they have given me.

My mentors Rohini and Himanshu. My life got a whole new direction professionally after meeting these two individuals

My manager at my first company, Pooja Rana, gave me the task to conduct sessions on health and fitness across the different teams. This kickstarted my journey of excelling in public speaking and it was something that I enjoyed. And I can say by taking those sessions I discovered my passion.

Preface

I have been keeping notes about my personal experiences with communication and I am finally ready to share some of them publicly.

My contribution is to find the ideas that matter the most and connect them in a way that is highly achievable.

The evolution of communication is an ongoing process. Despite the world of the web has bought individuals closer, the connection has to be rekindled at multiple levels. This book intends to dig deeper into the roots of communication by focusing on how one can be more assertive and empathetic while communicating.

The backbone of this book is the seven different aspects of communication- public speaking, emotions in communication, social awareness, power distance index & mitigated speech, silence, assumptions in communication and lastly building connections through communication

Each chapter advocates its relevance under the umbrella of communication through stories, case studies, real-life examples, tools, and techniques to overcome problems in communication. The stories, facts, case studies, experiments, and data shared in the book are from credible sources.

The chapter on public speaking highlights the history of public speaking which dates back more than 2500 years and talks about the first speech textbook published on papyrus written by a man named Corax who laid the foundation of expressing views through speech making for thinkers like Socrates, Plato, and Aristotle. It also talks about overcoming nervousness and other problems associated with public speaking through simple tools and techniques along with real-life examples, case studies, and activities.

The chapter on emotional intelligence is designed to educate the readers to understand the origin of their emotions and strengthen their abilities to understand the emotions of others as well as acknowledge differences. The part of social awareness is intended to teach the readers to be better at communication in a social setting by helping them develop skills that include identifying social cues, taking others' perspectives, and demonstrating empathy and compassion.

The subsequent chapters of the book cover the concept of mitigated speech and its relevance while communicating with people of higher power like superiors, leaders, or clients. The first half, emphasizes the need to understand the impact of age, gender, culture, and social status on speech and how unconsciously these factors impact our communication in a negative way. The tools and techniques to avoid the overuse of mitigated speech are also shared for better clarity. The second half of the chapter concentrates on the role of countries in shaping our communication by understanding it through the Power Distance Index data and how it has negatively and unconsciously impacted the effectiveness of communication for people living in different countries. It attempts to enable the cultural understanding of the world and its effect on communication by highlighting a few real-life examples of renowned people pointing out how culture influences the words we speak and our behavior.

The latter part of the book talks about a very powerful form of communication- 'Silence'. How being silent can at times work in your favor and at other times against you. This chapter is shouldered with articles, real-life stories, and events related to the topic. It also comprises the methods and practices to use 'silence' in favor of one.

Another chapter is devoted to one of the most crucial facets which influence communication way before the actual communication starts. And that is how our own assumptions sabotage effective communication in the personal and professional domain. The real-life examples and stories will enable the readers to see how easily communication can be distorted by our failure to be mindful of our own beliefs and how they affect the suppositions we reach. Furthermore, it elucidates how skillful communicators probe their own assumptions and challenge them.

The narrative arc of the book is conveyed by real-life examples, engaging stories, original research, case studies, tools, and techniques that are easy for the user to understand.

The chapters include relevant illustrations of the literary work of prominent individuals like Rabindranath Tagore, Amartya Sen, Malcolm Gladwell, Leonardo da Vinci, and many other influential authors, for the readers to make it more relatable. The underlying idea is to simply connect.

In this book, after spending hours of researching I attempt to deepen my knowledge of several concepts as well as connect with my readers to help them overcome the blocks that they face in communicating at the workplace, in educational institutions, or in their relationships to help them shift their perspective in a positive way by covering crucial concepts through the different chapters.

By the end of the book, readers will be able to sail through the troubled waters of communication by:

- Collaborating more effectively with others by building high trust relationships of mutual understanding
- Assessing paradigms and aligning to aspects of communication shared in the book

The differentiating factor about this book is that many books that are available in the market, related to the same topic, talk about the surface-level problems that are related to communication and provide a quick fix to improve them. For instance, the best-selling book "How to Talk to Anyone" by Leil Lowndes. One of the highlights of the book is, 'that anything you say is fine as long as it is not complaining, rude or unpleasant.'

Honestly, it is not fine!

The receiver of the message may still get offended if his triggers are clicked due to an unpleasant experience in the past related to the topic which another person is speaking about with utmost politeness and by not being rude/complaining in his tone. The topic can be about marriage, job promotions, etc.

For instance, someone sharing the news of his relationship in a polite and enthusiastic way may not end up pleasantly in the mind of the person who has just signed his divorce papers and lost the custody of his children. In another case, a person who has got fired from his organization may not consider the news of someone else's promotion in a good spirit.

No matter whatever positive topic you chose, there is the chance that it may affect another person in a negative way. In such a case, one should be socially aware enough to pick up the queues from that person's expression and make the adjustment in his communication accordingly. This communication strategy is well explained in the chapters related to emotional intelligence and social awareness.

Other chapters in the book have inputs that have not been shared before.

For example, the chapter on public speaking talks about the history of public speaking which dates back more than 2500 years and shares a story of a kingdom where land was allotted to people who were able to make their claim for it through their speech and not by the land titles as they were destroyed by the dictator. A group of 500 lottery-selected jurors gave citizenship to the people who argued cases before them and gave the best speech as a part of their civic duties.

The book uses a simplified approach to help the target audience be eloquent in their speech.

Introduction

In the year 1990, A Columbian Airline flight destined for New York, crashed; killing 65 of the 149 passengers on board.

Avianca flight 52 was a regularly scheduled flight from Bogota to New York City.

Upon investigation, many reasons for the crash were ascertained and a few among these were the communication problems that had occurred.

Recordings suggested that the co-pilot had failed to convey the severity of the airline's low fuel situation. The co-pilot was using mitigated speech — a term made famous by Malcolm Gladwell, author of the book blink as well as many others as well. We will talk about mitigated speech in detail in the later chapters.

In short, mitigated speech is a linguistic term describing differential or indirect speech, inherent in communication between individuals of different hierarchies.

For example, the difference in speech when you are talking to your manager versus when you are talking to a worker who is working under you.

Talking in a commanding tone with a manager may not come as easily to many. No policy restricts you to do so if the manager himself is doing it. But sadly, our conditioning does. It is more of a query when talking to the manager, and more of a command when talking to a co-worker. People at such levels often develop a hard skin for their communication style when it comes to interacting with those working under them. Politeness has lost its meaning in a world that is moving at an extremely fast pace.

Something similar happened here, which you will be able to figure out from the transcript of the flight.

Because the entire transcript is quite lengthy, I have only put in a particular part here which is necessary to raise the alarm for the inappropriate communication that was made regarding the emergency of fuel exhaustion.

Avianca flight 52 had been holding pattern over New York for over one hour due to heavy fog limiting arrivals and departures in and out of John F. Kennedy airport.

During this hold, the aircraft was exhausting its reserve fuel supply, which would have allowed it to divert to its alternate, Boston, in case of an emergency.

Here is the transcript from Avianca 52. The plane is going in for its abortive first landing. The issue is the weather. The fog is so thick that both the pilot and his co-pilot cannot figure out where they are.

Pilot: The runway! Where is it?

Co-Pilot: I don't see it! I don't see it!

Pilot: Give me the landing gear up. Landing gear up

Pilot: Request another traffic pattern.

Co-pilot: maintain two thousand feet, one eight zero on heading

Pilot: Tell them we are in an emergency.

Co-pilot: That's right to one zero on the heading, and ah, we'll try once again. We're running out of fuel.

ATC (Air traffic control, NY): Okay.

Pilot: What did he say?

Co-pilot: Maintain two thousand feet, one eight on the heading. I have already advised him that we are going to attempt again because we now can't.

Pilot: Advise him that we are in an emergency!

Pilot: Did you tell him?

Co-pilot: Yes sir.

Co-pilot: I have already advised him.

Pilot: Advise him that we don't have fuel.

Pilot: Did you advise him that we don't have fuel?

Co-pilot: Yes sir, I have already advised him, hundred and eight on the heading. We are going to maintain three thousand feet and he's going to get us back.

Pilot: Okay.

The captain is desperate. "Tell them we are in an emergency!"

And how does the co-pilot communicate with ATC? "That's right to one-eight-zero on heading and 'Ah' we will try once again. We are running out of fuel."

Running out of fuel is not an SOS term when it comes to declaring an emergency.

All the planes as they approach their destination are, by definition, running out of fuel.

The co-pilot here, we can say, was ambiguous in his communication because he was not able to clearly communicate that they didn't have enough fuel to make it to the airport.

Also, how the co-pilot described the emergency is something to put focus on here.

The plane is dangerously low on fuel and the co-pilot begins with the routine acknowledgment of instructions from ATC, and doesn't mention his concern about the fuel until the second sentence.

Also, his inserting the 'ah' filler in between sentences undercut the importance of what he was trying to say.

Upon investigation, another controller who handled the flight that night mentioned that the co-pilot spoke in a manner that conveyed no emergency.

The reason for this unhurried and unconcerned manner of speech from the co-pilot could have been because of two things: First, he was trying to communicate the airplane's fuel situation in the best possible way known to him, and that can certainly involve his inability to communicate the message in the way it was required to be; and second, he was trying to be overtly polite as there is a chance that he might have been intimidated by the guy from New York ATC, who was at the other end of the phone and was trying not to offend him with a stronger speech. A researcher who was going through the plane crash investigation did mention that the New York air traffic controllers are famous, or in this case infamous, for being rude, aggressive, and bullish. Such things can also be noted in day-to-day communication at workplaces. When managers are aggressive/bullying they, intentionally or unintentionally, bring down the factor of psychological safety when it comes to team members raising the issue for important things or things that are bothering them. Cultural differences can also be a factor when it comes to the way two people communicate with each other. One person's natural style of speech may seem to be rude to someone from a different culture. Even our interpretation of someone's comment and our emotional reaction to it based on our conditioning and past experiences can also change the meaning of the message being communicated. We will discuss such things as well as many others related to communication in detail in the following pages.

In the Avianca airline crash, communication error was the significant factor that led to the crash. The same was published in many reports and had also become the headline for many newspapers including the L.A Times.

Now imagine yourself in a similar situation where your hesitation and nervousness restrict you in putting across your message in the right way. Like the above example of an airline crash, there can be two factors to it — internal and external. What one would like to focus on are internal factors, as that is the area where we can do adjustments in order to deal with external factors. Obviously, to some extent, we can do adjustments to the external factors as well. For example: if someone is being rude to you at your workplace, then you can always voice your opinion to that person for the same.

"If an egg is broken by an outside force, Life ends. If broken by an inside force, life begins. Great things always begin from the inside"

The Seven different chapters are portrayed as troubled waters in this book where one finds it difficult to make out from the current of the stream if you are the one in charge of the boat.

The stream is so strong that you let it direct you to a destination instead of you dictating your own way.

At times, you may end up alive on the shore without any serious injuries, and on other times, you may hit a rock and end up severely injured or even dead at the shore or you may also probably sink.

But if you are a skilled captain who knows the waters and is a mindful thinker who can stay calm during such instances then your chances of coming out of such powerful current streams are exponentially higher.

Such powerful current streams of the sea can be a perfectly normal thing for you if you are facing such kind of a situation on a day-to-day basis.

You will be able to sail effectively if you can understand the troubled waters and yourself.

Communication under the aspects shared in this book can be related to such troubled waters that a sailor has to tide over on a daily basis.

It will be a challenge for those who think that, when in that kind of a situation, it will be the currents and not them that will chart the route to their destination.

Here, in this book, the challenges one faces in day-to-day communication and the solutions for these challenges have been shared.

Based on what people hear as soon as we begin to speak, they decide whether they want to listen to what we're saying or give credence to our point.

Be it an interview, a speech, your big break, or a difficult conversation - all of that hinges on our communication.

Communication is certainly not about being fluent in English. It is more about connecting with your audience in any language which both of you can understand.

It is about speaking the right words at the right place at the right time and unambiguously.

It is sharing what's on your mind eloquently without getting swayed by emotions. People having proficiency in a particular language can't always be called good communicators as we are aware of instances where such an individual tends to sit quietly during tough conversations or when something stupid is being said or talked about by an individual higher in authority or social standards or even equals.

I hope you will take advantage of the advice and suggestions shared here in this book.

I would also suggest you go back and reread the chapters that interest you.

Honestly, the swiftness with which we forget things is quite surprising.

To remember what you have read, you need to keep going back to it again and again.

I advocate all the material shared in this book but at the same time, I will be honest with you and say that you may find it difficult to apply every one of these suggestions all the time because most of us lose touch with these things once we have read them once.

I find it difficult sometimes to apply everything that I advocate.

For example, when you are frantic it is much easier to complain and condemn than it is to try to understand the other person's viewpoint.

I keep on posting quotes on my Instagram page. One quote I posted about was *moving at your own pace and not comparing yourself with others.*

A couple of days after posting it, I accompanied my wife for her driving session. She drove quite well but when it came to parking the car,

she took some time. I was frustrated and shouted 'it doesn't take that much time.'

At the same time, a car driven by a lady went by us.

I asked her to see how easily that lady was driving whereas she was taking such a long time to do it.

My wife was irritated and reminded me of my post regarding *Moving at your own pace and not comparing yourself to others.*

It felt like I had hit a brick wall face first. It was a harsh realization in disguise. So, to cut the story short, we all can fault at things about which we advocate.

A yoga instructor can forget his instructions if he often skips his practice.

A motivational speaker can run out of motivation if he doesn't flex his brain muscle on the topic regularly.

A guitarist may find it challenging to hit the right cords if he doesn't pick up his guitar and practice regularly.

In the end, no matter what craft is your specialty, it may fade away the moment you stop paying attention to it on a regular basis.

Hence, with patience and practice, you can get better at communicating effectively.

Content Of Chapters

1) A way with public speaking

- Bid adieu to the dreams
- Be nervous be very-very nervous
- Even the best speakers were scared once
- Myth about public speaking
- No one way to success
- Take care of your voice
- Pictures running through people's mind
- What's your point?
- Actions speak louder than words
- How to stay calm before the big talk

2) Role of emotions in communication

- Controlling your emotions while communicating
- Self-inflicted emotional scars
- Laugh off the negativity
- Take control of your self-talk
- Harvard study on EI

3) How being socially aware can help

- Zoom out
- Triggers in your way
- Let's understand ourselves first and then others
- Continuing a conversating with the dis-interested ones
- Make It Safe for Them Not to Answer
- Cold communication can get you in trouble
- Recognizing the mood of others

4) Mitigated speech and power distance index

- What is mitigated speech
- Chaos under stress

- PDI – Power Distance Index
- How your country may impact your communication

5) Silence

- Why do we choose to remain silent when we witness something wrong?
- Academic scores are not communication scores
- When to zip your mouth
- Depart from the accepted standard by acting deviantly
- Build a coalition

6) How assumptions affect communication

- The problem with assumptions
- How Intentions play a part
- The inner filters
- So how do geniuses handle it
- Assumption that we make or self-image that we have created
- How limiting beliefs affect communication

7) Communication is connecting

- Make connections like the poets of Iceland
- Breaking the ice
- Inferiority/Superiority
- Hell, or heaven
- Stay away from toxicity
- Let's get out of this ditch together
- Take a compliment
- Building rapport through mirroring
- Connecting with people at all levels
- You are safe with me

CHAPTER I

A WAY WITH PUBLIC SPEAKING

BID ADIEU TO THE DREAMS

At the age of 13, accompanied by my father on his gray Bajaj Priya scooter, I went for trials of the under-14 national cricket team at the national stadium in New Delhi. We reached at around 9 AM and I saw a queue of more than three hundred other kids just like me who had come for the trials. After waiting for almost 4-5 hours under the scorching sun, my turn finally came!

We were supposed to pad up and bat at the nets. My initial worry was not the balls I would be facing but the fact that I didn't bring the abdominal guard with me. It is supposed to protect your manhood from leather balls approaching you at a high speed. Anyway, I went inside the nets to bat and face the bowler who was giving his bowling trials.

His parameters to get selected was to bowl in an economical way or, even better, try to get me out while mine was to play the ball as perfectly as I could, preferably hitting some shots. Six balls were all that one was given to play.

As I took my stance in the nets, I could see that I was surrounded by a hundred or so kids around the nets, who were waiting for their own turns. They had their eyes and attention glued on the individual in the nets.

At that time, it was me.

1st ball went like a rocket past the stumps and I couldn't touch it.

2nd, 3rd, and 4th had the same fate.

I was not being able to connect them with my bat.

The 5th & 6th balls did connect, but with my leg pad, not with the bat. Six balls were suddenly over and I was not able to connect to a single delivery. I was shown the exit for the next individual to come in. My dreams were shattered that day and never again was I able to muster the courage to try

1

once more. For middle-class families – we prefer to play safe rather than take a risk.

Playing safe was to concentrate on studies, get to college, get a job, and get married. All of which I obediently did. But what was there on the field that I was not able to perform that day at the national stadium? For earlier, during a practice session in school, I had performed exceptionally well in the nets while facing much better bowlers.

I believe the reason that I was not able to perform that day was not that I lacked skill, but it was because I was surrounded by people who had their eyes on me and were expecting me to perform. The issue was the people around me and my interpretation of the situation, not my skills or the lack of them.

The issue today is similar when it comes to speaking in front of a crowd. We are more concerned about the crowd, although most of the time they do nothing but just stand there and watch us. However, just their presence impacts our communication negatively. It is our interpretation of them or what they might be thinking is something that impacts our performance.

That is what fear of public speaking is.

It is not about the fact that you can't speak in front of people. It is more about the concern that people are watching you and your interpretations about it that instill fear in you. It was not the skill that broke my childhood dream of playing for the country but the lack of confidence to stand there in front of people and perform that killed it. This lack of confidence and inferiority complex continued to haunt me for a long time. I never participated in any stage shows or cultural activities during my school or college days. No debates, no street plays, no singing, dancing, etc. I must say that I just survived school and got out from there.

Graduation days followed in the same fashion with no participation in any extracurricular activities. Once I did gather the courage to take part in a fashion show but backed off at the last moment. I just didn't have the courage to walk in front of others. Honestly, I was even scared to walk in front of three or four people that were auditioning at that time.

Then I enrolled in MBA. At first, I fought with my mother to not pursue MBA. But now I see it as a blessing in disguise as it brought me in connection with my wife, Ruchika, and also made me realize the importance of having good communication skills.

In most MBA colleges, you are required to give presentations.

It was the same in my college as well. It was my first time giving the presentation in front of the class and we were supposed to do it in groups of four to five. My friend Abhinav prepared the presentation content of about four pages and handing it over to me, asked me to memorize it. I thought it was going to be easy. I just had to memorize, go out there, and speak. So finally came the day of the presentation and I was prepared, or so I thought.

As our turn came, we stepped in front of the class packed with 60 students in attendance; all waiting patiently for the speaker to arrive. My turn came to present my part. As I stepped in front of the class and started speaking, I felt a phenomenon that you get when you get nervous.

My palms were getting sweaty.

Legs were trembling.

My voice was shaking.

My heart was like a bullet train.

Similar things happened back at the national stadium when I was 13.

I was running out of breath. In short, I was feeling suffocated because I was experiencing stage fright. Words were coming out of my mouth but in bits and pieces. Certainly not how I had expected them to come out.

And the other students were having a hard time understanding what I was saying. Just within 2-3 minutes of the presentation, I stopped abruptly and said in a hurried tone, "Now my friend will continue with the presentation."

At that time, I just wanted to move away from the limelight. My part was remaining but the courage to fulfil it had flushed out of me. Two years passed by like this and I avoided every such situation to give a presentation. When there was no way of avoiding it, I tried vodka to upscale my courage and confidence level. Yes, it worked but it also made me feel more miserable and vulnerable when the next time I had to present and vodka was not handy.

But then came a time when I realized that this was not the way out of it and I can't be dodging off every time an opportunity would knock and I may be required to speak or present in front of an individual or a group. Hence, an urge to learn the art of public speaking was the first thing I started when I joined my first company. Yes, it is an art! It needs to be practiced like any other art form.

Today you can see many people sharing their content and offering training on public speaking communication. But let me tell you it is not something that has just popped out of somewhere and has created a demand for itself recently. It has a history and dates back to over 2000 years!

Let me give you a peek into the history of public speaking and why it is a must for us to master this trait of communication.

Over 2400 years ago some of the people living along the Mediterranean Sea began to set up the first democracies ever known in the world. They lived in small states. These people – like all others in the world back then – were ruled by one kind of dictator or another.

But now they started overthrowing these dictators and began to rule themselves. Soon, however, they made a discovery — they could not rule without establishing a structure of speechmaking.

For example, one person after another would come to a new democratic government and say, "Five years ago the dictator seized my land. It's my land. I want it back."

The dictator, of course, had destroyed all the land titles, so the new democracy had to create a jury system to find out who really owned the said land.

These juries consisted of 200, 500, and even 1,000 men. There were no lawyers. Each citizen contended his own case. He had to stand up before these large groups of men and describe why the land he claimed was really his. To his disappointment, he found that truth and justice were not enough. He might tell the truth, and his cause might be just, yet the jury would not trust him, or even understand him. He needed speaking skills. The man who gave the best speech invariably got the land.

They also needed speaking skills in their new legislatures. When the 500 or 5,000 freemen assembled to pass their laws, citizens might say, "We need a firm new law."

But they could not get a new law just because they required it.

Someone had to stand up and make a whole lot of freeman hear him effortlessly, occasionally with the winds blowing and other noise drifting in from the outside setting. He had to know how to get their attention and win their goodwill, so they would want to listen. He had to explain his case clearly, so they would remember it. He had to answer questions skillfully. These things he had to do, or else he could never get a new law!

At once, people in these primary republics were required to study speechmaking. Within ten years the first speech textbook was published – on papyrus, of course, for there was as yet no paper and no printing press.

The book was written by a man named Corax.

Corax invented some of the elementary principles and laid the foundation for the Greek scholars to follow – particularly Socrates, Plato, and Aristotle. They took these properties and applied them to other rhetorical uses, particularly in government. However, Corax developed these methods specifically for the law court, not the assembly.

Under the Deinomenids, who were there on the Greek mainland in the early fifth century BC, the land and property of many common citizens had been seized; these people flooded the courts in an effort to recover their property.

Corax developed the art of rhetoric to allow ordinary men to make their cases in the courts. His chief contribution was in helping structure legal speeches into various fragments: poem, narration, statement of arguments, refutation of opposing arguments, and summary. This structure is the foundation for all later rhetorical theories.

He was the originator of the system of speech making, the first who laid down the rules for effective speaking.

All of this, of course, denotes how the study of speechmaking got started. The speech itself is as ancient as the human race. Simple speech forms were used by primitive men before he discovered fire, long before he learned to write or even to draw with a stick. This, in short, has been the history and the relevance of speech making.

People were scared back then and they are scared today as well when it comes to standing up in front of an audience and communicating their point. The way I was able to figure out the problem of conquering the fear of the public's presence and learning the art of public speaking was by going through it. I started speaking wherever and whenever it was possible. Be it social gatherings or huddle time in the office.

Along the journey, there were people who supported me and encouraged me to go on. Rohini and Himanshu, my trainers at my first company, were among them. Honestly, there were also people who laughed and ridiculed me when I was trying initially, you may encounter these kinds of people as well, but for me, that was fine because I had shifted my attention from them towards my goal of becoming better at communication.

It is believed that when one is driven by a purpose then external factors are least weighed upon. Only the internal work is done.

Public speaking is listed as the number-one fear, before death, which is at number five, and loneliness, weighing in at number seven. I guess that means that most of us are less afraid of dying alone than of making fools of ourselves speaking in front of others.

I honestly don't see public speaking as the number one fear among the others on the list like death!

What if someone puts a gun to your head and gives you a choice to either speak or get your brain blown out by the bullet. What will you choose? Certainly not the second one!

Fear is a powerful motivator for leadership, which means that you stand above the crowd. There is the fear of being seen as exceptional and different, the fear of the unknown, the fear of being a fraud, the fear of forgetting everything you were going to say, the fear of being at risk publicly; and the fear of being up there, alone.

They all come together, for most of us, in public speaking.

I believe I was able to achieve some control over it, as in my office I was asked by the department head to take communication sessions for my colleagues. I was supposed to go to different teams and make a pitch about the sessions and ask them to participate in them.

I was quite successful with my pitch. Almost 70-80 percent of team members out of a crowd of more than 300 nominated themselves for the session, which ran for over three months, in different batches.

I still have the feedback form of all the participants which I cherish to this day. As one of the feedback items read that the best part about a 9-hour shift at the office is the one-hour session we get with you.

It was all fun and learning for both me and the participants.

I can never say that I have arrived at a place where my role is only to impart training. For me, it will always be a bilateral process of learning.

I made mistakes. I learned the process and I am still learning and I still make mistakes. In the end, it doesn't matter what the world thinks about you. The only thing that matters is how you see yourself and where you want to lead yourself.

Anyone can develop any specific set of skills by just being consistent.

"It is not the critics who count, not the man who points out how the strong man stumbles. The credit belongs to the man who is actually in the arena; whose face is marred by dust, sweat, and blood, who strives valiantly, who comes short again and again. Because there is no effort without error and shortcomings; but how knows great enthusiasm who spends himself in a worthy cause.

Who at best knows in the end triumph of high achievement and who at worst, if he fails, he fails at least while daring greatly"

- Brene Brown

BE NERVOUS. BE VERY VERY NERVOUS

Being nervous is completely fine when it comes to speaking in front of an audience. It is natural and one should be nervous.

Piyush Panday mentions a moment he had with Amitabh Bachchan when he was in Gujrat for shooting a TV commercial in the middle of the Gir forest. He was called to his room and made to listen to a recitation of his father, Harivanshrai Bachchan's, 'Madhushala'. He was reciting it in preparation for a recitation that he would do in Paris in the next few weeks, and although he had heard his father's recitation many times, he wanted it to be perfect.

This is the level of commitment one should aim for; he mentions.

Reciting it weeks before the actual event date, despite knowing it thoroughly, this is the type of commitment one should have before an event, be it a big talk or a one-on-one interview.

Now, talking about being nervous before the presentation. It is quite normal to be nervous. That is what Amitab Bachchan had underlined, in his conversations with Piyush Panday, in the latter's book, PANDEYMONIUM, that he is always nervous before shooting. Not sometimes, but always.

He further mentions, 'that the day you stop getting nervous, the day you think that you have arrived, is when the downfall begins.'

"There shall come a day in the life of every champion when they will realize there is another greater one around the corner"
- Amitabh Bachchan

EVEN THE BEST SPEAKERS WERE SCARED ONCE

Our father of the nation, Mahatma Gandhi, was among those individuals who had the fear of public speaking. On the British Councils' website, you will find that other famous figures like Abraham Lincoln and Warren Buffet, to name a couple, also, like Gandhi, suffered from the phobia of speaking in front of people. Gandhi's biggest asset was his voice. As he believed in non-violence, his voice was his only weapon. Everyone has a voice but does everyone speak when it is required the most.

Coming back to Mahatma Gandhi. He was a lawyer before becoming a reformer in India. In fact, he was a lawyer for 25 years. Mahatma Gandhi in his initial years had quite a shy sort of personality. The dreadful stress of public speaking became a problem so great for him that he even avoided speaking at friendly get-togethers and dinner parties. In later life, still, a lawyer, the fear of the mob continued to haunt him.

During his first case before a judge, he panicked and left the courtroom, feeling humiliated after not being able to think of any question to ask.

But he worked on it and overcame it. Before leaving South Africa, he gave up the practice of law and instead started giving speeches wherever and whenever possible. Mahatma Gandhi was able to overcome his worries due to finding a cause that ignited a passion that was bigger than any fear. In many books and surveys, I have read that public speaking is the no.1 fear that people have. I don't believe in such a statement and I would suggest you not to either.

Jerry Seinfeld is a successful celebrity and one of the richest actors/ comedians alive. Regarded as one of the 'top 100 comedians of all time' according to Forbes, he earned more than 200 million dollars in the year 1998. But his initial years were full of struggle as a public speaker trying to make a living by doing stand-up gigs.

In 1976, after graduating from Queens College, at the age of twenty-two, he tried his hand at standup during an open-mic night in New York City where he froze on stage, forgetting the joke.

From the second row, a jeerer asked, "Is this your first time?"

He was hooted off stage and felt dejected about the failure. But he didn't stop. He simply kept going. Though he had rehearsed his material thoroughly the night before, when he stepped out on stage, he couldn't remember a word of his act. "I stood there for about thirty seconds ... saying absolutely nothing, just standing there, freaking out. I just couldn't believe it," he had later said.

But this didn't pull back his confidence. He continued his spell of standup acts over the next three years which eventually led to an appearance on an HBO Special for Rodney Dangerfield and, subsequently, to a role in the sitcom, Seinfeld. He, in the true sense of this book, was able to overcome the troubled waters.

Any fear can be overcome by persistent efforts and this is what Jerry was able to do. By his continuous efforts and not stopping after multiple failures, he was able to build an empire for himself.

Here's a piece of advice by him on public speaking;

"According to most studies, people's number 1 fear is public speaking and number 2 is death. Death is number 2, does that sound right?

This means, to the average person, if you go to a funeral, you are better off in the casket than doing the eulogy."

If you have a purpose in life and that needs to be done, even if it is speaking to hundred different people every single day for a year, then you will, with time and effort, be able to control your fear.

"The way you overcome shyness is to become so wrapped up in something that you forget to be afraid" - Ladybird Johnson

THE MYTH ABOUT PUBLIC SPEAKING

I read a statement in an article that it is all well enough if it so happens, for a speaker to have a pleasing voice, but it is not essential. This, though right in a sense, is deceptive and teaching of this sort may not be of assistance to young speakers.

The purpose should be to make the voice effortless. In the effective use of any other instrument, we apply the greatest skill for faultless adjustment or coordination of all means of control.

A tabla or a guitar if played randomly by a person without any knowledge of it will make an unpleasant sound. A musical instrument can produce melodious sounds if played in the right way and have the opposite effect if played in an incorrect way.

The same goes for voice. Since speech is to express a speaker's thoughts, training in speech should not be altogether distanced from training in thinking. Back when countries were run by dictators, the significance of training in public speaking was also at its peak.

Dictatorial countries used to give their leaders more careful training than democratic countries as free people were often careless in nature and were never able to understand the relevance of effective speech making while living in a free society. But dictators had to plan such things with care or their chances of perishing would cloud over their dictatorship. Hence dictatorial governments were often setting up party organizations to recruit and train 'personal oral agitators.'

The Soviet alone maintained a core of 3,000,000 trained speakers in its shops, factories, farms, and political subdivisions.

In today's world, it is commonly found in school systems that future leaders are not been given the opportunity to train in public speaking. Giving presentations doesn't count under the training of public speaking. It may improve your confidence but still, a lot of distance will be left to catch up with the skill of public speaking.

The schools are operated on the notion that "anybody can talk."

In the same sense, "anybody can do paper cutting." However, this is only half the truth. A child who can cut paper dolls cannot also cut intestines safely and surgically as a doctor can. There are various levels of cutting; some are easy while some are difficult. The same goes with talking. Mere chitchat is easy. But effectively speaking in public is difficult, about as difficult as removing a part of the intestine. The dictators back then knew this and mandated their people to be trained.

NO ONE WAY TO SUCCESS

We are regularly told by what means a few orators have succeeded, but we are barely ever informed of the causes from which many other speakers have been nervous or have failed. There are many books in which there is the argument offered about ways of succeeding by authors and most of the text from different individuals contradicts at some point or the other. In one book it may be written that a guy was able to succeed only by this or that means, therefore all should do as he did.

This seems very striking to read, for instance, that to succeed in speaking it is only necessary to know your material well.

But another writer points out that this is quite ridiculous. That many speakers have not lacked in this aspect and despite knowing their material they were not able to speak properly. If we want to row or sprint or play cricket, we do not simply go and do our extreme, we apply the finest technical skill to the art, we pursue to learn from the knowledge of the past and through the best teaching available.

If we want to get a job or pitch an idea, merely speaking out your plan or achievement may not help. However, effectively advocating them with conviction and better articulation can benefit one exponentially.

Let us see why, with this scenario;

A group of nine friends are appearing for an interview for the same job and with the same interviewer

1. Ravi goes to the interviewer and says, "I have a strong body and I am a willing worker." He gets the job with a certain salary.
2. Ashish goes to the employer and says, "I have a strong body and I am a willing worker. I am also an honest guy." Ashish gets a higher salary than

Ravi.

1. Abhay goes to the interviewer and says: "I have a strong body and I am a willing worker. I am honest and can plan my work to accomplish the most result in a short and effective time." Abhay gets a higher salary than Ashish.

4. Vaani goes to the interviewer and says: "In addition to the qualifications and skills of the first three, I like people and they in turn like me. They come to me for my advice as well. Vaani gets a higher salary than Abhay.

5. Raghav goes to the interviewer and says: "I have all these qualifications. In addition, I am good at inventing things. I can create new things that capture the interest of people, thereby creating new opportunities and jobs." Raghav Gets a higher salary than Vaani.

6. Shweta goes to the employer and says, "I have all the qualifications of the guys who came before me. On top of that, I have a productive imagination. I can create new ideas and put them into action.

I also have the skill of explaining them in a simple language so that anyone can understand them easily. She gets a higher salary than Raghav.

7. Vijay goes to the interviewer and says, "I also have all these qualifications. Additionally, I am a very good salesman. I know how to create a want in people to buy the things produced by the inventor. I also know how to answer their questions. I am also a good listener and have learned not to interrupt when another person is doing the talking." He gets a higher salary than Shweta.

8. Suraj goes to the employer and says: "I have all these qualifications. In addition, I am highly educated. I do not work by presumption. I hold knowledge on a wide range of topics and can explain it to others so that they can know what to do and what not to do, so as to have lakhs of rupees." Suraj gets a higher salary than Vijay.

9. Disha, the final interviewee, goes to the interviewer and says, "I have all the above qualifications. I also have a good understanding of people. I am

skilled in the tact of diplomacy and in the art of dealing with people. I am a socially aware conversationalist. Besides all this, I am an effective public speaker. I can talk not only to threes and fours but with a bunch of hundred people or more. I can explain ideas and articulate them in simple ways to colleagues, the board of directors, or the public. I can also listen to their ideas and criticize them with an open-mindedness and insight. I am therefore a proficient executive."

She gets the highest salary.

"He always avoided the man or the book that proclaimed one idea for correcting of society's ills"

Woodrow Wilson -28th president of US

The point is that a substantial amount of time is needed in communication like in any other teaching/coaching.

Time is needed for carefully working out a few essential principles, overpowering a few stubborn faults, and securing desired results by the right process through consistency.

TAKE CARE OF YOUR VOICE

The common trouble in using the voice for an intense form of speaking is the contraction or straining of the throat. This blocks the free flow of voice, causing an impaired tone.

For example, Narendra Modi and Rahul Gandhi are both in such a position that they have to often speak at events in front of large crowds. But it's very rare that we see any strain in the tone of Narendra Modi when he speaks whereas, a strain can easily be noticed in many of Rahul Gandhi's speeches.

Please excuse me here from the thought that I am indirectly sharing my understanding as to who is a better leader between them.

I am just trying to explain a point here without any intentions of comparing them in any sense.

The way to avoid broken control of voice is to learn at the appropriate time the general principles of what singers call voice production. The control of voice, so far as it can be a mindful physical operation, is determined mainly by the action of the breathing muscle. Breathing exercises are often prescribed for regular practice.

Such exercises, if done in an efficient manner, may be effective for vocals as well as beneficial to health. Moderately taking the breath at frequent intervals should become an unconscious habit. I practice the technique made famous by Wim Hof. Wim Hof (born 20 April 1959), also known as The Iceman, is a Dutch motivational speaker and extreme athlete famous for his skill to endure freezing temperatures. He has set a Guinness World Record for swimming under ice and continued full-body contact with ice, and previously held the record for a barefoot half marathon on ice and snow. He attributes these feats to his Wim Hof Method (WHM), a combination of frequent cold exposure, breathing techniques, yoga, and meditation. The Wim Hof Method combines breathing, cold therapy, and commitment to help you connect more deeply to your body. It involves powerful inhalation, relaxed exhalation, and prolonged breath holds. His technique is simple: take in a strong inhalation through the nose. Let out a relaxed exhalation through the mouth. Repeat for 30 breaths. On the 30th breath, exhale to 90 percent and hold for as long as you can. The technique can lead to:

- increased immunity
- better sleep
- reduced stress
- heightened focus

In 1995, Cornell University professor, Stephen Ceci, taught a developmental psychology course in the fall and spring semesters to about three hundred students each time. Stephen J. Ceci is an American psychologist at Cornell University. He studies the accuracy of children's courtroom testimony (as it applies to allegations of physical abuse, sexual abuse, and neglect), and he is an expert in the development of intelligence and memory. During the winter break that separated the two semesters, he worked to improve his presentation style. He received training to increase the variation of his tone of voice, to use more gestures while speaking and communicate an overall body language of enthusiasm.

When spring came, he delivered a course that was similar in content to the one he had delivered in the fall. Ceci and his colleagues even equated recordings of both sets of lectures to confirm that they were word-for-word copies. The only differences were the variations in his tone of voice and the addition of gestures. Other facets such as grading policy, assigned textbooks, office hours, and tests, remained similar.

However, the students rated all parts of the spring semester class and the instructor far higher than the class of fall. Even the textbook was rated better, gaining nearly 20 percent higher approval ratings. Spring semester students also believed they had learned far more, even though their actual performance on tests remained matching to the performance of the fall semester students.

Ceci himself was rated as more informed, more open to others' ideas, and better systematized even though, as he told himself, none of these aspects had changed from the previous semester. Studies have progressively shown that audience ratings of a lecture are more powerfully influenced by delivery style than by content. Your voice is crucial to communicating both warmth and conviction, but there isn't just one voice.

You can choose to play up different aspects of your voice depending on what you want to convey and with whom you're communicating.

Putting It into Practice: Voice Fluctuation

You can gain great understandings of your own voice fluctuation by practicing sentences with a recorder app on your phone. Repeat a sentence numerous times with as wide a variation in emotions as you can. Try to say it with anger, with sorrow, with authority, with care and concern, with warmth, and with enthusiasm.

Vocal Authority

If your goal is to communicate authority, set the pitch, tone, volume, and tempo of your voice in the following ways:

Pitch and tone: The lower, more resonant, and more baritone your voice, the more impact it will have.

Volume: One of the first things an actor learns to do on stage is to project his voice, which means gaining the ability to control its volume and aim it in such a targeted way that definite portions of the audience can hear it, even from far away. One exercise to improve your projection skills is to imagine that your words are missiles. As you speak, aim them at different groups of listeners. I am from a theatre background and have done many shows. A major chunk of what I have learned about voice modulation is through the training that was provided to me when I was doing theatre.

In theatre, the voice is imperative for both speaking and singing. With voices, performers communicate the dramatic truths of the characters through the dialogue of a play or the songs of a musical or opera. Breathing, resonance, and articulation are the fundamentals of vocal production and technique.

Tempo: A slow, measured tempo with frequent pauses conveys confidence.

Pausing is even more important when we want to give our audience time to reflect on what we have said. This is especially so when we make statements that may be intricate or even uncommon.

Pausing can indicate to the audience that you want them to think about what you have just said, without having to tell them to think about it. When using a pause for emphasis, you want to focus audience's attention on your most important pieces of information. Pauses regulate the rhythm of your speech like that of a natural conversation. They also help you collect your thoughts before moving on to the next piece of information.

Determine when and how long a pause should be to enhance your presentation. Typical pauses last one to two seconds; dramatic extended pauses last as long as four to six seconds.

"By your silence, ye shall speak."
-Rudyard Kipling

Putting It into Practice: Vocal Authority

The strategies below will help you communicate influence through your voice.

1. Speak slowly. Visualize the difference between a nervous man or a noisy child speaking at a high speed and the slow emphatic tone of a judge delivering a verdict. All three of them attract a different impact from their audience. For the nervous one, it is the least.

2. Pause. People who broadcast confidence often pause while speaking. They will pause for a second or two between sentences or even in the middle of a sentence. This conveys the feeling that they're so confident in their power, they trust that the audience won't interrupt.

3. Right breathing. Make sure you are breathing deeply into your belly and inhaling and exhaling through your nose rather than your mouth. Breathing through your mouth can make you sound breathless and anxious.

"The technique should not be too technical

That form should not be too formal
Teaching should not be too much "
- Philip brooks

PICTURES RUNNING THROUGH PEOPLE MINDS WHEN THEY ARE ASKED TO SPEAK.

They see themselves standing nervously in front of the crowd, perhaps having trouble remembering what they wanted to say. Run these images over and over again on your mental screen and you can be sure that you won't have much success as a speaker.

Instead, form a picture in your mind that you are confidently giving a presentation.

You look sharp. You deliver your lines smoothly. You tell a joke and your audience laughs. And at the end, you get a round of applause. Afterwards, people come to you and congratulate you. Vividly see the successful outcome of your meeting.

Remember that you are the producer, director, scriptwriter, lighting coordinator, costume designer, and casting director, of your own mental movies. You get to choose how they turn out by mentally rehearsing and running a successful outcome through your mind.

WHAT'S YOUR POINT?

The first thing of importance for the speaker is to find out the way to make himself clear as to his meaning.

The speaker has to ask this one question to himself over and over again – What is your point?

showing the picture:

At times, a speaker may see the picture in his own mind but how he articulates it to others doesn't reveal the point being made.

You may have clarity when you are writing but it is not necessary that it will come to your tongue when you speak.

A way to begin the speech is to make the voice sound like the things you are talking about. Some things are fast, some slow, some heavy, some light, some big, and some small. The wind blows, the ocean's level or it dashes high and breaks, happy things sing, sad things mourn.

And when our mental notions are put in real expressions or presented as a picture, how easy it would seem by this simple variation of voice to speak the language of that picture, enunciating the length, breadth, action, color, values, and the spirit of it.

But also keep in mind that you don't pay all of your attention towards showing the picture, such that the message gets hidden somewhere.

Many times, when we see an advertisement on television, we only remember the story of the advertisement but we forgot about the message for which the story was told. The speaker should keep to his central ideas, otherwise the speech will become dishonest and unreasonable.

Your story should be the envelope of the message and not the other way around.

ACTIONS SPEAK LOUDER THAN WORDS

Gestures simply don't mean the movement of hands and arms.

Many a times, I have seen speakers forcefully making gestures in their speech because they have read or heard it somewhere. And in turn, their gesture sets people off.

I remember one Toastmasters' meetings I had attended where a guy was giving a speech. Honestly, I have forgotten the title of the speech or the message that was being imparted through it. The only thing that I remember is that the man, in between his speech, was often patting his hand on his upper thigh. Yeah, that's the only part I remember because it was an awkward gesture and was totally not in sync with his message.

A thought, an emotion, something that moves the man from within, will cause a change; it may be slight or it may be very marked in the eyes, face, or body. One should learn to appreciate the idea which is being shared to see the full meaning of what he would say and specify by some general movement of body and expression of face, the changing moods of the mind. The amount of gesture is, of course, determined by the personality of the speaker, the nature of speech, the character of the audience, and the occasion of address. One speaker will, under certain conditions, gesticulate nearly at all times, another will, under the same condition, seem rarely to move in any way. The two may be equally effective.

A gesture is so largely a matter of the individual and is ruled so much by diverse motives and changing circumstances.

Finally, a speaker should remember that he goes to the stage, not to make a grand speech or receive praise, but because the podium is a suitable place from which to tell the audience something he has to say. Maintain an Open Posture while communicating as physical barriers are often some of the greatest interferences to connection for someone trying to communicate. It took me years to figure this out and to become more effective in my communication.

When I first started speaking to audiences, I usually stood behind a lectern and didn't move. As a result, I felt detached from the audience. When I started to walk around the stage and got out where people could see me, my connection with people enhanced greatly. Enter with simplicity, honesty, earnestness, and modesty.

Scott Berkins, the author of Confession of a Public Speaker, writes:

"Don't practice to make perfect and don't memorize. If you do, then you may sound like a robot or even worse. A person trying to say things in an exact, specific, and entirely unnatural style which people can spot easily.

The intent should be to know your material well so that you can be comfortable with it. Confidence, not perfection, should be the goal."

He continues...

"I repeat the process (practice) until I can get through the entire talk without making major mistakes. Since I am more afraid of giving a horrible presentation than I am of practicing for a few hours.

The energy from my fear of failing and looking stupid in front of the crowd fuels me to work harder to prevent that from happening.

It's that simple."

One should also keep an eye on expressions as well.

Develop Your Range of Expression similar to how great actors can tell an entire story without saying a word, simply by using facial expressions. Go and watch movies by Charlie Chaplin, you will understand my point. He made people laugh and cry and made them feel more human only through facial expressions.

Whether we are aware of it or not, we also convey messages with the expressions on our faces. Even people who work hard not to crack a smile or let others know what they're thinking are conveying a message to others – that they don't want to be engaged in a conversation; and that makes communicating with others nearly impossible. No matter who you are or with whom you are trying to communicate, you can improve your ability by smiling at people and being expressive. Even if you work in a tough environment or with a dull corporate, you don't have to maintain a grim appearance all the time.

How to stay calm before a big talk

This is a great exercise to use before any meeting or interaction where you want to feel confident. For instance, before a job interview or before meeting someone who you think is intimidating.

Follow these seven steps to convey confident body language:

1. Make sure you can breathe. Loosen any clothing if need be.

2. Stand up and shake up your body.

3. Take a wide stance and plant your feet firmly on the ground. A wide, stable stance helps you feel and project more confidence.

4. Stretch your arms to the ceiling, trying to touch it with your fingertips.

5. Now stretch your arms to the walls on either side of you, trying to touch them.

6. Bring your arms loosely to your sides, and roll your shoulders up and then back.

7. Inflate with breath and try to take up as much space as possible. Imagine puffing up like a gorilla, doubling in size.

Deborah H Gruenfeld, an American social psychologist and professor of organizational and social structure at Stanford University, found out that people who assume expansive poses (taking up more space), experience a measurable physiological shift.

In one experiment, assertiveness and energy-promoting hormones rose by 19 percent, while anxiety hormones fell by 25 percent. Assuming a strong, confident physical posture will make you feel more confident and more powerful. As you feel more powerful, your body language adapts accordingly.

Jordan Bernt Peterson (born 12 June 1962) is a Canadian professor of psychology, clinical psychologist, YouTube personality, and author. In one of his interviews, he talks about the importance of having a good posture. He says that people, in general, have very poor posture and that's very bad for them. In his book *12 Rules For Life: An Antidote to chaos*, there is a chapter where he talks about lobsters. In this chapter, he explains the fact that when a lobster loses a fight, which they are fighting all the time for dominance, they kind of crunch down and look smaller, and when they win a fight, they stretch out and look bigger. He further explains his point when he talks about lobsters, that lobsters run on serotonin neurochemical and if the lobster loses, the serotonin level goes down and if he wins, the level goes up. And when the serotonin level goes up, he stretches out and becomes a confident lobster. Serotonin is the key hormone that stabilizes our mood, feelings of well-being, and happiness. He further mentions that we have developed from lobsters from an evolutionary perspective some 350 million years ago and it's the same circuit. If human's serotonin level falls, we get depressed and we crunch forward and everything around us turns cloudy and black. We invite more depression and get into a bad loop. He suggests that if you are trying to get your act together, it's important to stretch yourself out and sit up properly or stand properly with your shoulders rolled back as it is a part of a psychophysiological loop that can start you on an upward curve.

I believe we can all probably relate to it. For instance, you had a bad day at work, your boss shouted at you or, as a kid, you were often bullied.

Then what happens is that our body posture changes. Straight shoulders become hunched and life seems to be gloomy and dull or depressive. And it expands into other areas of our life; disturbing our connection with family and friends. Having a good posture is like taking responsibility for yourself irrespective of whether the day has turned out to be good or bad. I don't mean to say that one should always stay positive, although it is advisable to try and do so. We can start small by taking care of our posture, which is quite a little thing to begin with but a very important one nonetheless, which often goes unnoticed.

Speech Day: Getting into the Zone

The single most significant guideline for a successful speech is simple: make it about them, not about you. As soon as you start worrying about yourself — speculate about how you're doing or if this or that sentence was good enough — self-criticism can easily arise.

If you can make it all about your audience instead —wondering how they're doing — you take the focus off yourself, boost your self-consciousness, and get into a state of goodwill, which will be appreciated by your audience.

Putting It into Practice: Speech Day

Arrive early if you can; walk the stage to visualize and own the stage. Visualize yourself giving a wonderful talk with confidence wherein your audience is liking it. Go into a quiet room nearby and use the tools of visualization to get into a state of confidence and warmth.

Pause before you start. Count till three, facing the audience, before you begin to speak.

During the presentation, assume things to go wrong — maybe an external distraction or you're fumbling on something.

Throughout your speech, remember to pause, breathe, and slow down. Don't run off stage; pause after your last words.

Here are a few activities that you can try to excel at the skill of public speaking.

Naming objects differently

This activity can be done in any classroom. In this, you have to name the objects differently.

For example: the table is not a table, it is a laptop, the fan Is not a fan, it is cooler, and so on, and once you do that you don't have to repeat the same name again for different objects.

Outcome – it helps you to add words to your vocabulary.

Imaginary gift

An activity between two individuals where A will give a gift to B and has to speak about that gift.

The gift will be imaginary. It will be on B to guess whatever gift he can perceive it to be and speak about it for 2 minutes and vice versa.

Outcome – improves impromptu speaking.

Spell everything you say

Activity between 2 participants.

In this activity, you don't have to speak words when you are making conversation. You have to spell your conversation.

Outcome – Increases focus.

Energizer

The first participant speaks a sentence and then the next participant has to make a sentence from the last word that the first participant spoke.

Outcome – improves impromptu speechmaking.

Alternative movie ending

Think of a television/movie story, narrate the same story to the class, but suggest an alternate ending.

Outcome – boosts creativity.

CHAPTER II

ROLE OF EMOTIONS IN COMMUNICATION

"Emotions can be the enemy. If you give in to your emotions, you lose yourself. You must be at one with your emotions because the body always follows the mind"

-Bruce Lee

CONTROLLING YOUR EMOTIONS WHILE COMMUNICATING

Excessive emotions either clog off the expression or run away with themselves. Being calm and poise is a state for good accomplishments of any kind. You need to learn to connect with people emotionally if you want to communicate effectively.

John Kotter, an author, in his book titled *A Sense of Urgency*, states, "For centuries, we have heard the expression, 'Great leaders win over the hearts and minds of others.' Note that he didn't say that great leaders win over the minds of others. Nor did he say they win over others' minds and hearts.

The heart comes first. And if we desire to be good communicators, we need to always keep that in mind. If you want to win over another person, first win his heart, and the rest of him is likely to follow.

A lot of speakers and teachers rely too heavily on their intelligence to persuade others. In addition, many of them also miscalculate people's natural receptiveness to the message and their desire to change because of it. These speakers and teachers believe that all they need to do is lay out a rational line of reasoning and people will be won over. It just doesn't work that way.

Therapist and leadership expert Rabbi Edwin H. Friedman remarked,

"The immense misunderstanding of our time is the assumption that insight will work with people who are unmotivated to change. Communication does not depend on syntax or eloquence, or rhetoric, or articulation, but more on the emotional context in which the message is being heard. People can only hear you when they are moving towards you, and they are not likely to do that when your words are hunting them. Even the choicest words lose their power when they are used to overpower. Attitudes are the real figures of speech."

Whatever is inside of you, whether positive or negative, will eventually come out when you are communicating with others. The proverb "As a man thinks in his heart, so is he" really is true; that comes across and impacts the way others react to you. People may hear your words, but they feel your attitude.

That will either permit you to connect with people and win them over or it will distance them and cause you to lose them.

In fact, your attitude often overpowers the words you use when speaking to others.

"The exact words that you use are far less important than the energy, intensity, and conviction with which you use them."

- Anonymous

People may hear your words, but they feel your attitude.

People who are able to connect with others on an emotional level often have, what could be called, presence or charisma. They stand out in a crowd. Other people are drawn to them. Self-mastery and enthusiastic spirit must be learned in order to become really strong. This is achieved by not trying hard but by relaxing. In case you are giving a speech, it should be brought down to the utmost simplicity and naturalness, so that the flavor of literature can be expressed with reality and truth.

Try adding stories to your communication style.

Brain scans reveal that stories excite and engage the human brain, helping the individual connect emotionally with others; making it much more likely that they will agree with the speaker. A college or school class is always interesting when your teacher is a good storyteller and can connect their stories with topics to magnify their communication.

I have been to training sessions extending up to nine hours a day.

Trust me, in some of these sessions, I felt like running away just after sitting through it for an hour, because it was only theoretical and there were no humor or stories in it at all. But, on the other hand, some sessions are such that you ask for more even after sitting for nine hours straight. If you have watched the videos of comedians such as Abhishek Upmanyu, Abhinav Bassi, and more of others like them, then It'll not be hard to guess why their videos have garnered so much many views on YouTube. It is because of their storytelling style.

Bryan Stevenson, the speaker who earned the longest standing ovation in TED Talks history, spent 65 percent of his presentation telling stories.

Stevenson talks to many people who have made up their minds to disagree with him well before he says a word. Narrative storytelling helps break down the wall between him and the people he needs to persuade. Narrative communication is a way of communicating through telling stories. Most often, narratives are used to recount a story or, in other cases, to express an opinion or give information to circumscribe a situation like past events from the perspective of the storyteller.

Implementing storytelling in your communication can be tricky. For some, it can be difficult to identify the areas in which effective storytelling can take place. For others, it can come naturally to them.

The best way to begin storytelling in your communication is to develop a strategy and the key message you want to convey. Friendly stories are great as they work to get the listeners into an active state of mind. A story that garners strong emotions is one that will last the longest in the mind of the listeners. For example, if you use storytelling to communicate a happy message or an emotional story, it will have bursts of joy or a sense of empathy or sadness. A story that engages many of the listener's senses, is the one that lasts.

A different type of story which allows the listener to feel as though they are part of the story themselves or they can relate to the story is the kind of story that can prove to be more effective.

Maxwell Maltz in his book, Psycho-Cybernetics writes:

"When in a situation where you have to speak in front of people, different people may experience the same situation in different ways.

Four people may view the same situation differently, as they don't share the same experiences. They also may not share the same emotions running through their mind when in such a situation.

Some would feel excited, some would feel nervous, and some would be stressed out, and so on. He continues that the external world is the projection of your internal state. You act and feel not according to what things are really like, but according to the image your mind holds of what they are like. You have certain mental images of yourself, your world, your experiences, and the people around you; and you behave as though these images were the truth, the reality, rather than the things they represent.

Five years before publishing one of the most influential books of the 21st century, J.K Rowling was living on welfare and struggling as a single mother. Rowling wrote the first book in the Harry Potter series while working the night as a teacher, but the copy was rejected twelve times by the publishers.

When *Harry Potter and the Sorcerer's Stone* eventually got published, Rowling was advised not to quit her day job since her chances of success were slim. But with over 450 million copies of the Harry Potter books sold, the failure predictions certainly turned around. Some would quit after a single rejection was thrown their way and others would go on, and move forward, by taking learnings from their rejections. Your emotions become a driving factor here, they decide the route for you, whether you will continue or surrender.

Arunima Sinha had tasted success in becoming a national volleyball and soccer player in India. On April 12, 2011, while Arunima was on a train, some robbers attempted to steal her belongings. She fought back and battled, but the robbers eventually pushed her out of the train. She remembers seeing a train moving towards her, but she couldn't get up in time. Her left leg was run over by the train, crushing it below the knee. After being quickly taken to the hospital, doctors tried to save her leg, but it had to be amputated.

Inspired by Indian cricketer, Yuvraj Singh's successful battle with cancer, Sinha decided that she was going to do something with her life. She took up mountaineering classes and did well in them. Upon her brother's encouragement, she decided to scale Mount Everest. On May 21, 2013, Arunima Sinha became the first female amputee to reach the top of Mount Everest. Any adverse story can be turned into a success story. It's just about how an individual perceives himself or herself.

SELF INFLICTED EMOTIONAL SCARS

Many people who have never suffered physical injuries have inner emotional scars and the result on their personalities is the same. These people have been hurt or injured by someone in the past.

To guard against any future damage from that or any other source, they form a spiritual shield to protect their ego. This shield helps them to protect themselves against any such event in which they experience a threat that some of those things could happen again. If you have been hurt at some point in life, then there is a great chance that it will spill its beans over you throughout your life, at times in tiny bits and at other times in large heavy chunks. This mostly happens in the case of people who were bullied during their childhood. Later on, in their lives, there are chances that they become anxious and can again get easily bullied. They get into a habit of shielding themselves every time they sense even the slightest danger.

For example, in the movie '12 Angry Men, which is one of the highest-rated movies of all time, the story revolves around twelve jury members discussing a case verdict where a boy is accused of stabbing his father to death. All the jurors are required to come to a common understanding. If all twelve decide that the boy is guilty, then he will be executed by an electric chair. The characters in the movie had no names and were referred to by numbers or their occupation.

Juror no.1 is an assistant high school American football coach. Juror no.2 is a meek and pretentious bank worker. Juror number 3 is a businessman and rather distraught father, opinionated, disrespectful, and very angry. Juror no.4 is a rational, analytical stockbroker, who is focused on facts. Juror no.5 is a man who grew up in slums. Juror no. 6 is a house painter, tough guy, blue-collar, very principled, and respectful. Juror no.7 is a wise-cracking salesman. Juror no. 8 is an architect and he, by large, is the protagonist of the film, and the only one proposing an argument that the boy might not be guilty. Juror no.9 is a wise and observant senior who gives the benefit of the doubt. Juror no.10 is a garage owner, pushy, loudmouth, as well as very bigoted. Juror no.11 is a European watchmaker, who became an American citizen, very polite, very wise. Juror 12 is a wise-cracking advertising professional who flip-flops in his decision between guilty and not guilty.

In the preliminary vote, all jurors vote 'guilty' except for juror 8, who argues that the boy deserves some deliberation. This irritates some of the other jurors. Especially juror 3, the distraught father. Juror 8 tries to prove his point by rationally going through all the evidence provided in the case and argues that reasonable doubt exists and that he cannot, in good, conscience, vote 'guilty'.

Juror 8 suggests a secret ballot from which he will abstain and agrees to change his vote if the others unanimously vote 'guilty'.

The ballot is held and a new 'not guilty' vote appears.

An angry juror 3, the businessman and distraught father, accuses juror 5, who grew up in a slum, of changing his vote out of sympathy. But it was not juror 5 who had changed his vote. It was the wise old man, juror 9, who had changed his vote and voiced it as well. Juror 8, the protagonist, makes further claims that the evidence that has been provided in court is not as it seems and most of it is made up by the eye-witnesses. Now juror 11 also changes his vote.

With time and further discussion throughout the movie, the rest of the jurors turn their vote from guilty to not guilty. Leaving just one still voting for guilty – juror 3, the businessman. The angry Juror 3 shouts that they are losing their chance to burn the boy. When juror 8 accuses him of being a sadist, juror 3 lunges at him and yells, "I will kill him" while another juror tries to calm him down.

Juror 3 gives a long and increasingly tortured string of arguments, building upon earlier remarks that his relationship with his own son is deeply strained, which is ultimately why he wants the boy to be given the verdict of guilty.

Though it is a fictional story, it is nonetheless quite relatable.

Here emotional strains inflicted in the past have caused one person to decide on a crucial verdict emotionally and not rationally.

At last, he finally loses all his grip on his temper and, tearing up a photo of him and his son, breaks down crying before ultimately changing his vote to not guilty, making the verdict unanimous.

Our emotions attached to our past experiences play a significant role in the present and future events. Therefore, it is important to be aware about it and not let them direct you in an irrational way. Emotional events of the past hijacks our rational thinking which leads to irrational decision and communication.

I believe this is the most perfect movie ever made that teaches us the value of human life and how our emotional past including experience, conditioning, etc. prevents us from thinking objectively in the present and future.

Another area where it can be related is bullying. The damage caused by bullying can continue, even after the bullying has ended and it becomes an emotional scar, which a person carries with them throughout their life. Jordan Peterson explains it better in his writing when he says, *"In the simplest of cases, the formerly lowly person (the one bullied) has matured and moved to new and more successful places in their lives. But they don't fully notice. Their now counterproductive physiological adaptions to an earlier reality remain, and they are more stressed and uncertain than is necessary. In more complex cases, a habitual assumption of subordination renders the person more stressed and uncertain than is necessary, and their habitually submissive posturing continues to attract genuine negative attention from one or more of the fewer and generally less successful bullies still extant in the adult world. In such situations, the psychological consequence of the previous bullying increases the likelihood of continued bullying in the present (even though, strictly speaking, it wouldn't have to, because of maturation, or geographical relocation, continued education, or improvement in objective status.'*

Performing in front of an audience can be one example for the same. You may have been speaking, and someone would have had passed a comment to you afterward that it may not be your cup of tea, and you held on to it, and whenever a situation comes up to speak in front of an audience, you may become defensive and reticent.

Now, let us talk about how emotions impact communication. We fear as we speak in front of people when the stakes are high. Fear, like the other 12 emotions according to discrete emotion theory, is the one we encounter the most. Or if a recent study is considered by the University of California, Berkley, 27 distinct categories of emotions can be identified.

Therefore, it is very important to know how emotions work. As it holds a direct impact on our communication. The better aware we are of it, the more control we can have over ourselves and how we communicate and react to external events.

WORLD – A series of positive, neutral, and negative emotions.

The events happening around us are neutral events.

It is our mind that correlates positive or negative aspects to it. Our conditioning plays a role here. Someone being outspoken and honest may attract fewer friends and more enemies.

For some individuals, if a person is speaking about a problem honestly and is truthful about it, then they might be considered a negative personality and for some, it may be the other way around.

THOUGHTS – We interpret the events with a sense of thought that continually flows through our minds. This is called inner dialogue.

We think big. We think out loud. We think outside the box. We think on our feet. Some studies say that our thoughts are connected to our physical experiences.

University of Toronto psychologist, Spike Lee, puts it as, "Bodily states aren't some extraneous thing – they're part of the thinking process."

In one study, Lee and a colleague exposed volunteers to different odors. They found that getting a whiff of a fishy odor aroused a feeling of suspicion. Likewise, when research participants were exposed to another person behaving suspiciously, they were better able to detect fishy scents.

MOOD – Our feelings are created by our thoughts and not the actual event. A person may recognize something that prompts a shift in their mood such as a stressful event at work. People may even experience changes in their mood if they have an underlying mental health issue. An impromptu request to speak in front of a group of people can send chills down the spine. You may be knowing what you have to speak about but would panic by imagining yourself making errors in front of an audience. Being calm can help you think clearly in such situations.

Janice Marturano, the founder of the Institute for Mindful Leadership, explains to senior leaders that when you are facing a stressor or the fight or flight instinct in your brain, the simple antidote is to take a minute and have a breather — redirecting your feelings to your breath or the feeling of your hands on your lap or your feet on the ground. This way you can bring your mind to the present moment. The small act of mindfulness halts the hijacking of the brain by the amygdala and can enable an individual to return to clarity.

For those of you wondering what emotional hijacking is, it is a term coined by Daniel Goleman in his 1996 book *emotional intelligence and why it can matter more than IQ.*

An amygdala hijack is an emotional response that is immediate, overwhelming, and out of measure with the actual stimulus because it has triggered a much more significant emotional threat. But being mindful about it during a stressful situation can help you get out of it.

This is what surfer Bernard 'butch' Connor JR. did to get himself out from a deadly shark attack.

Bernard was about to paddle into an approaching wave when he heard a strange splash. Over his right shoulder, he could see the fin of a shark coming out of the water about three feet away. The shark came straight for his left leg and collided with the thigh. At such a moment you know you are about to get eaten. He was terror-struck. He tried hard to paddle away but was unsuccessful. He was not able to think clearly as he was afraid and horrified. The shark kept mauling his foot. It could sense his fear, just like people can sense your fear when you are nervous. Even a monkey or a dog can sense your fear when you walk in front of them nervously. Under such a situation, blood doesn't circulate properly. The same happened with Butch at that time. There was less energy in his hands and legs due to his ongoing terror. He understood that the only way to deal with this situation is to stay calm and his body, fortunately, listened. He stopped trembling with fear.

With a calmer mind, he was ready to paddle towards the shore. And after five minutes of paddling furiously towards the shore, he made it.

People were awestruck and patted him on his back. For Butch Connor, standing on the surface never felt that good. It was not only a fight between man and beast, but there was another fight that was going on inside him with his behavior and his emotions. With great effort, he was able to calm himself down. For most of us, we won't ever have to fight a shark, as Butch did, but our brain does fight with such emotions on a daily basis.

Sometimes a simple thing such as breathing right can help one a lot as when we take a shallow breath, the brain gets deprived of oxygen which can lead to the inability of thinking clearly. Breathing practices are an amazing way to become more in touch with your mind, body, and spirit. Deep, conscious breathing can be used as a tool to stay in the present moment. Your mindful breath can also be used to feel the energy of your emotions, especially the uncomfortable ones that you may try to avoid. During stressful instants, conscious breathing allows you to shift and release negative energy instead of storing it in your body. This is important because stored-up energy often manifests as muscle tension and other physical ailments.

Even if such things don't help immediately and things go bad (though honestly, they work if you are a regular practitioner), then give yourself some time and have some patience. This is what Leo Tolstoy had said in his book, War and Peace, that time and patience are two of the strongest warriors.

Give yourself an extra day, a week, or a month to digest the bitter or stressful experiences. This will help you stay in control of your bad emotions. My first presentation experience at my post-graduate college was a sour fruit to digest and for a week I locked myself in my room thinking that I was the most useless individual in the world.

But then, as I gave it some time, and thought about it after a gap of a few days, the self-loathing lessened and a more rational view of my own self returned.

LAUGH OFF THE NEGATIVITY

Did you know that laughing and smiling sends a communication to your brain that you are happy? Our communication gets hampered a lot when we are filled with negativity and our loved ones are impacted most of the time due to it. If we assume the worst of people, our communication becomes defensive which, in turn, impacts our relationships as well. If we are in a good mood and smile a lot then the same thing shines through our face-to-face or telephonic conversations, and even emails.

The same is the case with scowling, a bad temperament, or a negative attitude. They will accordingly pass the message in various modes of communication.

Spiritual wisdom teaches us that positivity is the true nature of oneself.

To have negative values and attitude mean that we are going against the true inner nature of ourselves. Communication requires openness, honesty, and integrity; virtues that are linked with positivity and we should strive towards cultivating and sustaining them. Negative values and attitudes will only impair communication, for negativity affects communication by halting it entirely or severely restricting it.

In such situations, when you are stuck at a distrustful or negative thought, forcing yourself to smile helps you counter your emotional state.

In a research performed at the University of Clermont Ferrand, in France, two groups of subjects read the same page from a comic book. One group was asked to hold a pencil in their teeth because it activated the muscle responsible for smiling.

Those who were unknowingly smiling found the cartoon more humorous than those who were not. If you are asked by a researcher to move your facial muscles, one at a time, into a position that would look sad to an observer, you will report sad. If you are asked to move the muscles one by one into positions that look happy, you will report feeling happier. Emotions are, in part, bodily expressions and can be amplified or dampened by that expression.

Even Charles Darwin, in his groundbreaking book, The Origin of Species, suggested that the act of smiling actually makes us feel better. So next time when you are nervous, worried, or in a bad mood, force yourself to smile and it will trick your brain to change your mood for the better.

TAKE CONTROL OF YOUR SELF TALK

According to research done in Queens University, Canada, the average person will typically have more than 6000 thoughts in a single day.

If the majority of your thoughts give you a message that you are bad when it comes to communicating with people, then there are high chances that it will become the case, even if you are not.

In a study done about thoughts, by The University of California, Davis, the struggle of two boys and their ability or inability to counter their thoughts were explained.

Boy A and Boy B were both struggling with math' get a D in their test. Boy A gets a D, gets angry, feels frustrated, and negative self-talk enters his mind. He says to himself that he is worthless, and that no matter how hard he tries, he is destined to fail. He communicates with himself over and over again in a negative way. As a result, a surge of negative emotions mounts over him and at once, he feels helpless.

A few years later, after completing his schooling, he doesn't get into college which he had dreamed of because he had set a belief in himself that he was an average student. He gets a job that he hates and considers this to be his irreversible fate.

Now let us talk about BOY B

He is the one with emotional intelligence and awareness. It's the same situation and same grade; he gets a D as well. But before his negative emotions can take over, he sits back, takes a few deep breaths, and thinks about his conditioning on how to control his emotions, especially the negative ones. He was taught to think about one thing that he is grateful for during such difficult times of stress and anxiety. He was taught about gratitude.

'Recognize all you have to be thankful for during the worst phases of your life.'

He remembered that positive gratitude can become reflexives that get built up in the brain if practiced regularly, and people with these reflexives, when hit with waves of stress, can better manage their stress levels and therefore, their lives.

The boy, now aware of it and with his newly built confidence, tries his hand again at math.

This time he gets a B which makes him realize that he is in control of his life and his emotions. He is successfully able to cope with the negative beliefs by communicating with his inner self in the right way.

I remember appearing for my first job where I got selected as a sales trainer. I was having a conversation with the recruiter and we were discussing some of the past interviews that I had given, and one of them was for AmEx(American Express). He told me that with my communication skills it was difficult to get into a company like AmEx. I accepted the fact that I did not have very good communication skills back then, but I never bought the belief that this was something that was fixed and I would never try for that interview again, just because of the disparaging comment that was made to me. Two years later, I cracked the interview but couldn't join them as my company didn't release me on the timeline given by AmEx.

Honestly, had I believed, truly believed, that this company was out of my league, I would never have tried or even thought of trying myself out at the interview. Many of us set the same belief for ourselves, which is quite alarming and not at all true and can be changed with consistent efforts.

According to Daniel Goleman, impactful communication is an effective give and take. It is an exchange between two or more people who contribute to the conversation. It is the ability to clearly state what we want, to communicate our needs and our motivation. Emotional intelligence is the ability to recognize our own emotions and the emotions of others, as well as the capacity to manage these emotions so that they don't have an impact on our behavior. There are many things in emotional intelligence that can help you to be effective in communication, for emotional intelligence teaches you to be aware of yourself and to be in control of yourself.

It allows you to stay cool and composed during the heat of a particular moment.

One competency of emotional intelligence is empathy which allows us to keep an inquisitive mind and stop ourselves from judging another person too quickly when we are communicating with them.

Empathy enables you to adapt your verbal and body language according to that of the person you are communicating with which, in turn, helps to build a rapid connection.

The deepest form of understanding another person is empathy. Empathy involves a shift from observing how you seem on the outside to imagining what it feels like to be you on the inside, enveloped in your skin with your set of experiences and background, and looking out at the world through your eyes. Psychologists have found that each of us is more interested in knowing if the other person is trying to empathize with us — whether they are willing to put in the struggle to understand how we feel and see how we see — than we are in believing that they have actually accomplished that goal.

Empathy is one of the significant gears of emotional intelligence and can have an incredible impact on how we communicate in all situations. Empathy demands from us to know the situation of the other person and understand the feelings of that person under a particular situation.

For example, your friend might seem upset with you for no reason. The first thing that you must do in such a situation is to think about what they must be going through.

Consider the circumstances that may be affecting their emotions and how that might, in turn, affect or dictate what they say to you.

Learn to engage with others by using the following.

- I am sorry I wasn't aware of that and if you could tell me more about it, I will see If I can help.
- That's something new for me. Let's discuss it in a more in-depth way.
- How do you feel about that, and what are your concerns?
- Correct me if I understood it wrong. Here is what I heard you say.

There is an assumption that our intelligence or academic score is related to how well we can communicate. But that's not true.

Studies have shown that people with higher emotional intelligence are better at communication. If you have been good at academics, you can probably be doing well when it comes to intellectual contribution but not necessarily in communication.

On October 23, 1990, David Pologruto, a high school physics teacher, was stabbed by a very smart student of his called Jason Haffizulla. Jason was not a teenager you'd think would try to kill someone. He consistently scored 'A' grades and was determined to study medicine at Harvard. But this was his collapse. His physics teacher gave Jason a 'B', a mark Jason believed would be a dent in his entrance to Harvard. After discovering his B, Jason took a knife to school and stabbed his physics teacher, before eventually being restrained after a struggle.

Two years following the incident, it was reported in a New York Times article that Jason had raised his grade average to 4.614 (exceeding the perfect average of 4) by taking advanced courses and graduating with the highest honors. He was smart. He got better-than-perfect grades and still lost himself emotionally by trying to wound or kill his teacher. He could, of course, never have improved his grade by stabbing his teacher. Then how come someone as smart as Jason does something so dumb?

The answer is simple — *Smart can be dumb*. Studies show there is little to no correlation between academically intelligent people and emotional intelligence, and that smart people are as likely to be good at communicating as "dumb people". Smart people with poor communication skills often make some common mistakes in their communication. Intelligence can also, at times, work against you. Students are often shocked to learn upon graduation that their technical qualifications are not as important as they'd thought.

Students in school are often led to believe that their academic knowledge is the primary factor to get a great job and success.

Howard Gardner in *Frames of Mind: The Theory of Multiple Intelligence*, defines various types of intelligence and emphasizes that schools are too focused on logic and linguistic intelligence.

Robert Kiyosaki in *Rich Dad, Poor Dad* is a famous author who argues against the common belief that the government's education system leads students to wealth and success.

Malcolm Gladwell's *Outliers* contains further proof that such intelligence has little correlation with achievement.

Graduates enter the workforce only to realize that their co-workers hate them, less intelligent people are the ones receiving promotions, and sucking up to the boss doesn't help in personal earnings. The students have "hard skills" such as technical know-how, but they lack the "soft skills" like communication or conflict management and social etiquette. A person's knowledge can be useless in some industries when that person has no people skills or, we can say, communication skills required to deal with people on a day-to-day basis. You can have great ideas, theories, and solve complex problems, but if you cannot effectively communicate that material in a persuasive and exciting manner by relating to your fellow human, you face an uphill battle in whatever challenges you encounter. It's not that people dislike you because of your intelligence; it's just that people dislike you because you're rude, not understanding, or annoying to be around. An intelligent person with poor communication skills can be insensitive, unapproachable, and therefore, uncommunicable.

Academically intelligent people fail in predictable areas of their lives for predictable reasons. What makes matters worse is that they avoid solving the dilemma because of their pride. The *genius-failure paradox* describes that people who want to feel smarter, wealthier, or generally superior to others refuse to seek help in dealing with people. You can feel dull learning a skill like communication that you believe should be natural. To learn such a skill may be an admission of your weakness and stupidity. But one thing we do know is that communication skills need to be frequently practiced.

While some people can naturally have the gift of being a good conversationalist or being emotionally intelligent through their conditioning and experiences or having the trait of easily winning friends through their communication skills, but for those who lack these and fall face-flat during such moments, being emotionally aware of your communication and behavior should be at the pinnacle of yours must know skills. Poor communication skills can put one in a risky cyclic effect, for poor communication prevents you from confronting or embracing situations that require those skills, further decreasing your social skills.

If a boy has poor communication skills during his developmental years because he did not participate in activities like stage plays, football, or anything else of that sort, then it can be a struggle for him to get out of the pothole of social awkwardness due to the cyclic effect of avoiding social situations. To be honest, this was the case for me as well and impacted much of my connections during my school and graduation years.

Things, however, started to change for me when I realized what I was missing and began to work on it. Things have improved for me over time but are still a 'work in progress' in many regards, and in a way, it is good to realize that communication is always a work in progress and something that keeps getting better with time. Because once you think that you know all that there is to know in the communication skill trade, then that day may well be the start of your downfall. Technical skills can help you secure your dream job or first promotion, but might not guarantee to progress to the next level as there is an emotional element that you need to consider. It is what helps one to successfully communicate effectively, manage stress, and connect with others.

HARVARD STUDY ON EMOTIONAL INTELLIGENCE

Harvard was sending their best and brightest students out in the work world but they weren't really succeeding in their careers. So, the university studied and researched the cause for it.

They found that there are 3 areas that matter for success

1)IQ

2)Technical skills

3)Emotional skillset

IQ and technical skills will get you inside the door, but EI proved to be twice the factor for success. 80-90% of our effectiveness as a good leader who can communicate lies in our EI skills. Be aware of your feelings, as our feelings play a huge part in the way we communicate.

Travis Bradbury and Jeon Greaves in their book, Emotional Intelligence 2.0, mention about an EQ test performed on those who took an online EQ test.

Only 36% were able to accurately identify their emotions as they happened. For example, we might get angry with a person but not fully understand that the reason for our anger has nothing to do with what that person said or did. Instead, we might be angry because we failed to see the other person's comment not as a form of criticism or attack but simply as a suggestion or new idea. If we are angry, sad, or afraid, we may be able to control our verbal communication, but not so much the nonverbal clues. This is where emotional awareness or the ability to understand and communicate our feelings will help. If you are emotionally aware, you will be able to notice the emotions of other people and how their feelings influence the way you communicate. Whether it is helping a stressed-out colleague or asking your boss for a promotion or raise, being emotionally aware will help you adapt to the course of that particular conversation. If your partner doesn't seem to be in a mood to talk about something, then you need to be aware enough to understand it and determine the best time to engage with them when they will be more receptive to what you have to say.

CHAPTER III

SOCIAL AWARENESS IN COMMUNICATION

"The beauty of social awareness is that a few simple adjustments to what you say can vastly improve your relationship with other people"
Travis Bradburry

ZOOMING OUT

Whilst having a conversation, in which you are talking to another person or group, you hear a remark that puts you off or sparks a bad feeling in you about yourself, what would you do?

Get up and deal with the remark by putting all your energy into that remark and getting distracted from the main topic? Or distance yourself from the remark? I think you'd want to choose the latter. It's always better to get disassociated from that remark and respond rather than react.

In other words, *ZOOM OUT!*

Our feelings about it will be a direct consequence of our own interpretation of the remark. Criticisms often have a greater impact than compliments and bad news frequently draws more attention than good ones.

The reason for this is that negative events have a greater impact on our brains than positive ones. Psychologists refer to this as the negative bias (also called the negativity bias), and it can have a powerful effect on your behavior, your decisions, and even your relationships.

Negative bias is our tendency to not only register negative stimuli more readily but to dwell on these events as well. Also known as positive-negative asymmetry, this negativity bias means that we feel the wound of a reprimand more powerfully than we feel the joy of a praise.

This psychological phenomenon explains why bad first impressions can be so difficult to overcome and why past traumas can have such long-lasting effects. In almost any interaction, we are more likely to notice the negative things and remember them more vividly later on.

For example, you might be having a great day at work when a coworker makes a lame comment that you find annoying. You then find yourself thinking over his words for the rest of the day. When you get home and someone asks you how your day was, you reply that it was terrible —even though it was overall quite good save for that one negative incident.

When such things happen, just 'zoom out' and apply these few strategies shared by Kendra Cherry, author of The *Everything Psychology Book*, to overcome negative remarks while you communicate with somebody.

Stop Negative Self-Talk

Start paying attention to the type of thoughts that run through your mind. After an event takes place, you might find yourself thinking things like "I shouldn't have done that" or "I shouldn't have said that" This negative self-talk shapes how you think about yourself and others.

Reframe the Situation

How you talk to yourself about events, experiences, and people plays a large role in shaping how you interpret events. When you find yourself interpreting something in a negative way, or only focusing on the bad aspects of a situation, look for ways to reframe the events in a more positive light.

This does not mean ignoring potential dangers or looking at things through rose-tinted glasses. Instead, it simply means refocusing so that you give fair and equal weight to the good events.

Establish New Patterns

When you find yourself reflecting on things, look for an uplifting activity to pull yourself out of a negative mindset.

For example, if you find yourself mentally reviewing some unpleasant event or outcome, consciously try to redirect your attention elsewhere and engage in an activity that brings you joy.

A few more ideas to get your mind off negative thoughts:

- Go for a walk.
- Listen to upbeat music.
- Read a good book.

Savor Positive Moments

Because it takes more for positive experiences to be remembered, it is important to give extra attention to the good things that happen.

While negative things might be quickly transferred and stored in your long-term memory, you need to make a little extra effort to get the same effect from happy moments.

So, when something great happens, take a moment to really focus on it. Replay the moment several times in your mind and focus on the wonderful feeling it evokes.

So, it is always important to keep in mind that the comment may not have been intended the way you heard it. Avoid engaging in a reaction that's going to shut down your curiosity and openness.

TRIGGERS IN YOUR WAY

I was reading a blog in which a guy wrote:

'My wife hates it when I raise an eyebrow at her when she talks. It literally makes her red. She gets extremely angry when I do it. We can be talking jovially and the minute I do it, her tone instantly changes and she fires off a warning, "Don't look at me like that."

The reason was totally irrational and illogical for me, but to her, it was a trigger and finally the reason for it revealed itself to me. Her parents used to give her that look when she was a child and she didn't like it.'

Remember a scene from the movie Golmaal where Ajay Devgn would get angry the moment someone showed him a finger. Yeah, that can also be called an emotional trigger. An emotional trigger is any topic that makes us feel uncomfortable. These emotional triggers are telling us which aspect of our life we might feel frustrated or unsatisfied with. It can vary in each person because we all are struggling with something different.

Being aware of it can help us take action to protect ourselves from reacting negatively when confronted with such triggers. Being aware simply helps us know our limitations and avoid, as much as possible, exposing ourselves to situations that hurt us and negatively affect our mental health and self-esteem.

It might, at times, be conversations or social media posts or it might be news or a song or movie and so on that sets off emotional triggers and impacts us and our communication with friends and family when we are with them.

For example, there might be a situation when a close friend or relative shares some exciting news about themselves. You are happy for them but can't help feeling envious. It can be your best friend getting a promotion or, if you have ever noticed, it can be any topic of conversation that triggers you when you're hanging out with your friends or family.

For example, people talking about their promotion or how their jobs are good at providing them with benefits or their salaries, it can be anything. It is only you who need to answer this question, as to why they impact you. You don't have to run away or disassociate yourself from these conversations, rather embrace them and learn from them about the discomfort they cause, and work on it.

While some might be out of our control, it is also very important to be aware of the situations/people/conversations that we can limit our exposure to. The important thing about spotting and identifying your emotional triggers is that it can alert us about our own mental health and help us become more aware of ourselves. When we are more aware, we can begin to take responsibility for the way we manage our emotions, as opposed to letting them control us.

When we can't manage or process our emotions appropriately, we end up simply reacting to others.

The first step required here is to take stock of who you actually are.

You need to dive deep for that.

When you buy a second-hand car and prepare to drive it, you hire an inspector to list all its faults. You will even pay him for the bad news, because you need to know what fault is in the car, if any. There is an urge to discover the hidden flaws of the machinery. You need to know because you can't fix something if you don't know that it's broken. And honestly, most of us are broken and we need such an inspector. The internal critic could play the role and get one back on track only if you can cooperate and not lie to yourself. You must take a deep dive within yourself and listen judiciously to what your mind says and make adjustments accordingly.

Another takeaway from this is to be calm and to write down how it is impacting you. I would suggest keeping a journal and writing it on a daily basis. See it as a place to confess your struggles and fears without any judgment or punishment. Write down as descriptively as possible all the negative things that trigger your mind and how they impact you and why they impact you. Most importantly, do they impact you at all, or are they just occupying the space in your mind like a tenant, who never pays the rent, occupies.

Both should be thrown out as quickly as possible. Be calm and understanding and don't take things personally based on your triggers when communicating with another individual.

There are certain things that arouse a variety of emotions. Something might make you angry or envious. Something else may make you guilty or sad. Or, unlike your friends or close ones, it truly bothers you when someone asks you about your personal issues. For some, it's a question or conversation about money; for others, it's a romantic relationship; and for someone it may be something about their past, maybe a childhood phase, or something of the sort.

Not only is it important for us to identify our triggers, it is advisable to be aware of the triggers of others as well. If you are speaking to someone and you see them displeased with what you are saying or not paying attention to what you are talking about, then that can be a hint that something that you have said could be acting as a trigger for them.

It would be better, in such a scenario, to ask questions or change the topic altogether, if you are not comfortable with asking questions. If even that doesn't work, then the best option is to politely move away from the conversation and try another day.

LET'S UNDERSTAND OURSELVES FIRST AND THEN OTHERS

To understand others, we first need to understand ourselves. Each of us sees the world differently. Trying to understand the other person's story helps to know why people have different stories in the first place. Our stories don't just come out of somewhere and neither are they random. Our stories are built into ourselves, often unconsciously, but in a systematic way.

First, we take in information. We experience the world — sights, sounds, and feelings. Second, we interpret what we see, hear, and feel; we give it a meaning, according to our own understanding and experiences. Then we draw conclusions about what's happening. And at each step, there is an opportunity for different people's stories to diverge.

Where Our Stories Come From

Simply put, we all have different stories about the world because we each take in different information and then interpret that information in our own unique ways. In difficult conversations, we often only trade conclusions back and forth, without realizing where most of the real action is — the information and interpretations that lead each of us to see the world as we do.

There are two reasons why we all have different information about the world. First, as each of us proceeds through life — and through any difficult situation — the information available to us seems overwhelming.

We simply can't take in all of the sights, sounds, facts, and feelings involved in even a single encounter. We, inevitably, end up noticing some things and ignoring others. And what we each choose to notice and ignore will be different. And that is one of the things that makes a big difference in our interpretation of the world around us.

Second, we each have access to different information. We each notice different things. Ravi took his ten-year-old nephew, Rahul, to watch a movie, for example, the latest one, a Punjabi movie called 'Honsla rakh'. Sitting beside his uncle's seat, Rahul shouted with delight as Diljit Dosanjh, the lead actor of the movie entered. Afterward, Rahul exclaimed, "That was the best movie I've ever seen!" and emphasized more on how Diljit Dosanjh made him laugh throughout the movie with his acting and said the movie was amazing just because Diljit Dosanjh acted superbly.

Rahul, obsessed with Diljit Dosanjh as he now was, saw nothing else. His Uncle Ravi, a father himself of a four-year-old boy, on the other hand, complimented the acting of the child, who portrayed the role of Diljit's son in the movie. And credited the child actor's skills and emotions for the movie's success.

In a sense, Rahul and his uncle interpreted the success of the movie from a completely different perspective. Like Ravi and Rahul, what we notice has to do with who we are and what we care about. Some of us pay more attention to feelings and relationships while some care more for status and power, or facts and logic. Some of us are artists, some are scientists, and some are pragmatists. Some of us want to prove that we're right while some want to avoid conflict and smooth a situation over. Some of us tend to see ourselves as victims and some as heroes, observers, or survivors. The information we attend to varies accordingly.

In a more serious setting, Abhay and Somya, co-workers on an assembly line, experience the same dynamic. They've had a number of tense conversations about racial issues.

Abhay, who is from a general category background, believes that the company they work for has a generally good record of minority recruitment and promotion. He notices that of the seven people on his assembly team, two are Schedule Caste and one is Schedule Tribe and the head of the union is OBC. Somya, on the other hand, believes in the merits of a diverse workplace and has noticed approvingly that several people who have recently been promoted are male.

Shyam, who is an Indo-Nepalese, has a different view. He has been on the receiving end of unusual questions about his qualifications. He has experienced several racial slurs from coworkers. These experiences are prominent in his mind. He also knows of several minority colleagues who were overlooked for promotion and notices that a disproportionate number of top executives in the company are Punjabis.

Both Abhay and Shyam have some information that is shared, but they have quite a bit of information that's not. Yet, each assumes that the facts are plain and their views are reality. In an important sense, it's as if Abhay and Shyam work at different companies. We often go through an entire conversation — or indeed an entire relationship — without ever realizing that each of us is paying attention to different things, that our views are based on different information. In addition to choosing different information, we each have access to different information. For example, others have access to information about themselves that we don't. They know the constraints they are under; we don't. They know their hopes, dreams, and fears; we don't. We act as if we've got access to all the important information there is to know about them, but we don't. Their internal experience is far more complex than we imagine.

We Have Different Interpretations

A second reason we tell different stories about the world is that, even when we have the same information, we interpret it differently — we give it a different meaning. I see the cup as half empty, but you see it as a metaphor for the fragility of humankind. I'm thirsty and you're a poet. Two especially important factors in how we interpret what we see are (1) our past experiences and (2) the implicit rules we've learned about how things should and should not be done.

We are influenced by past experiences. The past gives meaning to the present. Often, it is only in the context of someone's past experiences that we can understand what they are saying or doing makes any kind of sense.

To celebrate the end of a long project, Suriya and her coworkers scraped together the money to treat their supervisor, Aashima, to dinner at a nice restaurant. Throughout the meal, Aashima did little but complain: "Everything is overpriced. How can they get away with this?" and, "You've got to be kidding me! Five hundred rupees for lime soda!" Suriya went home embarrassed and frustrated, thinking, "We knew she was cheap, but this is ridiculous! We paid so that she doesn't have to worry about the money, and still, she complained about the cost. She ruined the evening."

Though the story in Suriya's head was that Aashima was simply a miser, he eventually decided to ask Aashima why she had such a strong reaction to the expense of eating out. Upon reflection, Aashima explained, "I suppose it has to do with growing up as a child of a single parent. I can still hear my mother's voice from when I was little, getting ready to go off to school in the morning. "Aashi, there's one rupee on the counter for your lunch! She was so proud to be able to buy my lunch every day. Once I got to be around eight or nine years old, one rupee wasn't enough to buy lunch anymore. But I never had the heart to tell her."

Years later, even a moderately priced meal felt like an extravagance to Aashima when filtered through the images and feelings of her past experience.

Every strong view you have is profoundly influenced by your past experiences. Where to vacation, whether to slap your kids, how much to budget for your child's first school trip, these are all influenced by what you've observed in your own family and learned throughout your life.

We often aren't even aware of how these experiences affect our interpretation of the world. We simply believe that this is the way things are. Asking questions and being more understanding can help to fill this gap.

CONTINUING A CONVERSATION WITH DISINTRESTED ONES

Generally, you will find two types of people at a social gathering.

One guy will walk into a party and, if he lacks communication skills or social skills, might be incapable of starting an interaction with anyone by himself and withdraw into a corner hoping that someone will notice him. Or he may try to be lively and overly glossy, turning people off with inappropriate and shallow friendliness.

Another person with the right communication and social skills upon entering the room would shift his attention away from himself and will start talking to another person about the topic he perceives to be mutually agreeable.

If the feedback is negative, then he will try a different topic or, maybe, a different person. Such people are the life of parties. The one who continuously brags about himself is just the opposite and people usually distance themselves from such individuals. It is important to notice the response our efforts elicit when we talk to other people.

Ever noticed that, at times, when we are having a conversation with someone and they disengage, not giving you the attention, you expect from them. They seem to wander someplace else when you are talking.

When we are excited or feeling a bit desperate, we sometimes find ourselves trying to encourage or persuade others to listen to us.

This intense behavior sometimes pushes people away. Remember that the longer your explanation the lesser your influence. It is like a telemarketer who continues trying to pitch to you long after you have politely said No. To avoid this, pay attention to how someone is responding to you.

When you notice someone's lack of interest in a conversation, it's better to step back, stop talking, and let them lead. I once encountered a similar situation when I was talking to a colleague about a training that I was conducting. After talking for some ten minutes or so, I saw him look away disinterestedly. That was my clue, so I said, "Well, let's leave this for another time." I tried talking about his watch and he was still not interested. So, I stopped the conversation, passed a smile, and saying, "Let's catch up at another time," left from there. Remember that you will not always be able to crack a conversation or continue one, as there may be times when the person, you're conversing with would be in a different state of mind altogether and may not be interested to talk to anyone, no matter who is standing in front of him. When you get such a clue, just walk away.

According to an article on *WIKI HOW by Kelli Miller*, there are a few things that you can do to carry a conversation forward when someone is disinterested:

- Have some talking points prepared: - Whether you are going to a specific event where you will have to speak with people or you just want to be prepared to talk to anyone throughout the day, it can be very helpful to have some talking points ready.

I remember an instance from my job at a fitness center as a sales representative when I was being given training by one of the senior managers. Apart from providing some wonderful training, he always had some topics upon which he could speak and spark interest from others. From chocolates to the day-to-day design of normal things, he always had some topics on which he could crack and continue a conversation with almost anyone and everyone.

- Comment on a topic that is common to both of you: - As you ease into speaking with each other, focus on the things that you both have in common at that moment, like the room you are in, the event you are attending, or the place where it is located. You can also possibly talk about food. It doesn't matter where you come from, food is one thing that can keep people connected. While sharing a meal with colleagues or friends, spark an interesting conversation about food.
- Get to know the person by asking open-ended questions: - Whether you already know this person or you are talking with someone new, show your interest in another person and encourage them to participate more in the conversation. The best way to do this is by asking questions that cannot be answered with a simple yes or a no.

For example, you can complement someone about their clothes and ask them where they bought them from? Instead of asking, "Have me we met before?" Try saying, "I think we had met at Ravi's birthday party a few months ago. What have you been up to since then?"

- Avoid sensitive topics: - As you start a conversation with someone who has trouble carrying on, it is best to stick to a topic most people can contribute to.

You don't want to make the person feel uncomfortable or uninformed by talking about subjects that they can't or don't want to talk about. Avoid topics such as religion, politics, money, family problems, health problems, and sex.

- Listen carefully and give positive feedback: A very important aspect of being a good conversationalist is being a good listener. As you carry the conversation and encourage another person to talk, be sure that you are listening attentively to what they say when they do speak up. When they respond, give them positive feedback so that they are encouraged to continue joining in.

For example:

  - That's an interesting way of looking at it! I never thought of it that way before."

    - Wow! Where did you learn so much about cricket?
    - I have always wanted to learn more about that skill. Do you have any book recommendations?

- Thread the conversation: Another technique that has been mentioned in this article is to keep the conversation going, which is termed as threading the conversation.

This is where you dissect each statement a person makes into parts and then choose a particular part to follow up with to keep the conversation going.

This will help you to respond to their comments without coming across as interrogative. For example, if a person says, "I just got back from Germany and I am completely jet-lagged, but I am supposed to have a meeting tomorrow morning." You have three conversation threads to follow up with — Why they went abroad, the fact that their jet-lagged, and their job. You can choose any one of these threads and respond with a question or even an anecdote like, "I was in Germany last year, visiting family. I stayed in Munich, where did you stay?"

End the conversation with a positive expression about your interaction. When it's time for you to part ways, be sure to let the person know that you enjoyed talking with them. If you want to feel comfortable, let them know that they are welcome to talk with you again sometime and exchange contact information.

Try to say something complimentary as you leave and be sincere when you say it. For example:

- I have to go find my table, but it was really nice meeting you. Thank you for keeping me company in this conversation
- I enjoyed chatting with you, and I look forward to seeing you at the next conference!
- I really enjoyed meeting you and I will definitely look up that book you mentioned (In case any was mentioned or you talked about any).

MAKE IT SAFE FOR THEM NOT TO ANSWER

Sometimes even the most skillfully asked question can provoke defensiveness. You ask a question out of an honest care towards the other person and a sincere desire to learn but they react by shutting down, defending, counterattacking, accusing you of bad intentions, or changing the subject. One response is to say that you are just trying to help and that there is no need to be defensive, and then continue to press for an answer. But this can be perceived as an attempt to control them, provoking further resistance. It's better to make your question an invitation rather than a demand, and to make that clear. The difference is that an invitation can be declined without consequence. This offers a greater sense of safety and, especially if the other person refuses to respond and your reaction makes that okay, it builds trust between the two of you. Whether you are talking with your co-worker or your eight-year-old daughter, give them the choice of to answer or not. It increases the chance that they will respond, and respond honestly.

Even if they don't answer right away, they may do so later, after they had thought about it. Knowing that it's their choice highlights your caring intent and frees them to think about the question.

COLD COMMUNICATION CAN GET YOU IN TROUBLE

Studies have shown that surgeons that sounded the least concerned, which means they sounded more anxious, more dominant, commanding, louder, faster, less melodious (monotone), were the ones that were getting sued the most by their patients. Reports suggest that these surgeons were trying to come across as strong in front of their patients and were communicating in an authoritative manner.

For example:

This is the course!

This surgery is to be followed without any miss!

This procedure is the only procedure you will follow!

Only being commanding in communication and not being passionate or enthusiastic about your work can give out a message that you are heartless.

Decades-old studies have shown that primary care physicians who are sued less often are those who are more likely to spend time educating patients about their core, use humor and laugh with their patients.

Source -NY times

Malcolm Gladwell in his book, Blink, talks about an analysis of medical lawsuits. In the analysis of medical malpractice, it was determined that there are doctors who make many mistakes and never get sued while there are other highly skilled doctors who get sued quite often. Gladwell noted the results of a researcher's study of hundreds of conversations that were recorded between a group of physicians and their patients.

The doctors whose tones were dominant tended to be in the sued group.

The doctors whose voices sounded less dominant and more concerned tended to be in the non-sued group.

Gladwell concluded that it eventually comes down to a matter of respect and the simplest way that respect is communicated is through tone of voice. This rule applies in other areas of life as well.

Most relationships fail when the tone of at least one of the person's involved is dominant or less concerned.

In his book, *The Relationship Cure*, Dr. John M Gottman, who is an American psychologist and who has worked for over four decades on divorce predictions and marital stability, reveals that when it comes to evaluating the meaning of communication in a relationship, only 7% of that meaning comes from the spoken word, while 38% comes from the tone of voice in communication. Words that may seem neutral and innocuous can become annoying if spoken with a sarcastic, demeaning, or contemptuous tone of voice; causing the listener to feel offended and disrespected.

You want your listener to focus on your words, not be distracted by your demeanor. You need to learn how to watch your tone and use it to get what you want.

According to a 2015 study that examined hundreds of conversations from over 100 couples during marriage therapy sessions, the ability to watch one's tone came out to be a key indicator of relationship success. Over the course of two years, researchers from the University of Southern California, recorded hundreds of conversations from marriage counseling sessions. They then analyzed these recordings, concentrating on things like pitch, intensity, and even warbles in the voice that can indicate moments of intense emotion. They also looked at the impact one partner's tone of voice had on the other.

To compare the data, a separate group of experts analyzed the behavior of the couples, taking special note of positive qualities like "acceptance" or negative qualities like "blame." The researchers then tracked the couples over a period of five years to determine if there was any change in their relationship. What they found about the tone of voice in communication confirmed what many of us already know intuitively – that communication is not just about what you say, but how you say it.

And the data showed that studying the couple's voices, rather than their behaviors, better predicted the eventual improvement or deterioration of the relationship. (Source – Tony Robbins.com)

RECOGNIZE THE MOOD OF OTHERS

When you see someone getting anxious or being in a bad mood, you may be swift to judge that there might be some problems that they are be going through. Then we become a person who starts offering them our advice, when they don't need it at the first place. At times, healing for such a person may come when there is someone who can only just listen to them and not offer any advice of their own. It is better to understand how and why they are feeling a certain way rather than jumping in as a rescuer and providing unsolicited advice. Sometimes, you might just want to be a mirror to such a person and not a repairman.

A waitress knows precisely what each of her customers need. It can be a tricky task. One particular table might want to have their food served quickly, another table may want professional and polite service. Some waiters have learned to spot customers who may cause problems and serve their tables without much personal involvement.

Everyone is there just to eat and the waiters are there to serve, yet, there is so much going on just under the surface that makes every table unique.

How does the waitress then quickly size up the tables and know their needs? She has a high level of social awareness, a skill that recognizes the mood of other individuals. Social awareness is about looking outwards and appreciating others. To build social awareness skills you need to observe people. The waiter who suggests a better dish, the salesperson who goes the extra mile to offer you what you may require, the supportive team leader, and the executive that remembers your name, each of these people have one thing in common — they excel in social awareness. You will learn to pick up on body language, facial expression, posture, and tone of voice, if you have a good level of social awareness.

As not every situation demands a verbal conversation, some are best left silent. Also, there are times when the conversation doesn't go as planned; the person you are having a conversation with isn't talking as much as you expected them to or you are getting disinterested one-word answers.

This happened to me once when I gave a call to one of my close friends and he didn't sound as cheerful as he always did. I, on the other hand, was harping about a new venture of mine, only to know later from his wife that he had lost his first cousin to Covid-19. One should always keep some questions that they can use just in case you have to bail yourself out of any silent or awkward situation, which usually arises in family gathering or office meetings.

It can be something like:

What's your view on this?

Or as trivial as – the weather seems to be pleasant!

They can give life to a dying conversation or an escape route out of an uncomfortable one. If it is still dead air though then you might want to excuse yourself out of it.

According to Daniel Goleman, the most important competency associated with being socially aware is empathy, which we have talked about in earlier chapters. However, it bears so much importance in our life that I had to include it here as well to explain this point better.

Empathy: Understanding the other person's emotions, needs, and concerns. Awareness of social situations is about carefully considering what people want and planning to communicate with them in a way that is intended to meet that need. Great leaders and public speakers are skilled in this ability and it helps them build trust and rapport. Being socially aware is a natural response to people, taking their situation and needs into account as much as possible.

Recent research, reported by Time Magazine, finds that college students of today have less empathy — the ability to understand and share the feelings of others — than students of previous generations.
Digital communication, social networking, video conferencing, and other forms of new media are being blamed for this loss of empathy.

Empathy seems to be on a decline with social media. After all, it's much easier to say something negative about others if you don't have to say it to them on their face. And if you don't feel like engaging in someone's problems then you can simply log off or even 'unfriend' them. It's an easy option these days. The trouble is that when there is no empathy and we are not working towards understanding the needs of others, there is also a significant loss of trust. Because, when you respond to the needs and feelings of other people, you gain their trust.

Others might be considered insensible and insensitive, but you will be trusted when you're able to understand and respond to the needs and values of individuals, or of a group. This is true whether you're a salesperson dealing with customers or a leader in an organization. Empathizing with someone, and understanding their perspective, doesn't mean that you have to agree with their point of view. Empathy is about acknowledging the emotions of others, being thoughtful and considerate of their feelings, and making decisions that take those feelings into consideration. Social awareness is a natural response to people and taking their situation and needs into account as much as possible.

Managers and leaders are usually aware of such traits of empathy and sympathy, but when things get heated from one side and they are at the receiving end, that is the time when their true skills are tested. The one who is able to lead the argument by a continuous act of empathy becomes a step closer to mastering the art of communication under tough circumstances.

Social seclusion is one thing that has led to less empathy in communication these days. Digital communication, social networking, video conferencing, and other new forms of media, contribute to social isolation and are often blamed for the drop in empathy.

Social isolation can cause a lack of empathy.

Covid-19 has led us into a world where there is less of social interaction and more of isolation.

Isolation can have a weird effect on a person. Initially, the person can desire the comfort of another human being. After some time, they may fear it, and be willingly to pursue isolation. In an article by Yvonne Taunton titled *'How has Covid-19 Affected The Way We Communicate?'* There is a mention of Tim Levine, Ph.D., chair and eminent professor in the College of Arts and Sciences, Department of Communication Studies at the University of Alabama at Birmingham who explains how the novel coronavirus pandemic has affected the way we communicate and its serious impact on our everyday communication skills.

"The most obvious changes are that most of us now have less face-to-face, in-person interaction with others, and when we are face to face, we are wearing masks," Levine said. "We have less interaction overall with people outside, and we spend more time on Zoom, Skype, and other mediated platforms."

Levine says, health-wise, social distancing is for the best, but social isolation is not healthy in the long run.

"There is some interesting and important research on the effects of social isolation on communication," Levine said, "One impact is that the less contact we have with other people, the more we become suspicious of other people. This can make others more defensive and lead to a vicious spiral where isolation leads to suspicion, which begets defensiveness, which reinforces the suspicion and leads to further isolation as a self-fulfilling prophecy."

A lack of empathy for someone can follow as a natural consequence of this enforced solitude. It becomes very difficult to empathize with something we fear. There are chances that such circumstances can make one depressed and a depressed person will, of course, find it very difficult to muster the will or the energy to be empathetic. Someone with depression just wouldn't see the point of being empathetic.

That's why a lot of depressed people end up losing friends and alienating family. They just don't feel the need to participate in life, they don't feel the need to service the machine of communication. They, unfortunately, distance themselves from the very thing that can help them out of their depression, such is the nature of the illness.

Depression and isolation together is a recipe for a toxic mix that feeds off one another. Depression can cause a lack of care to communicate. This will ensure isolation. The isolation will cause the depression to deepen. As the depression deepens, the more isolated the person will become. And round and round it goes. Empathy doesn't even register on their sensor. If I don't really know what you are thinking and feeling, I will trust you less and isolate myself. More importantly though, when you respond to the needs and feelings of other people, you gain their trust. This is true whether you are a socialist dealing with the public or a leader in an organization. Social isolation has detrimental effects.

In an article published under Cambridge University Press Public Health Emergency Collection, it is mentioned that social isolation is linked with various physical and mental repercussions including high systolic blood pressure and an increased risk of heart disease. Both loneliness and social isolation have been associated with an increased risk for coronary artery disease associated death. Furthermore, research has shown that both loneliness and social isolation are independent risk factors for higher all-cause mortality.

The article also highlights some tips for dealing with social isolation.

- *Spend more time with your family.* Utilize opportunities offered by the pandemic. Before the pandemic, some family members may have been distracted by work and school commitments, but now they may have more time at home and a higher degree of freedom to connect with loved ones.

- *Maintain social connections with technology.* Along with the telephone, technology has changed the way people interact with each other. Social media platforms such as Facebook, Skype, Twitter, Snapchat, and Instagram enable people to stay connected in a variety of ways. Many older people, however, may not be very familiar or proficient with these new technologies, and this style of interaction may not effectively serve their emotional needs. We can help older family members and friends to overcome such technological barriers. Online video chat is easier to use and sufficiently conveys nonverbal cues so that people can feel more engaged. Even without new technology being available, communication through phone services is beneficial too. Conversations with a regular schedule through online or phone services with family members and loved ones can be helpful for older people.

- Structure every single day. To stay confined at home for much of every day is a psychological challenge for many people. When most outdoor activities are not available, it is not easy to maintain a regular daily schedule. Make a list of things that you will do on a daily basis. It can be a small task or goal. Such things can keep one engaged throughout the day and can prevent negative emotions from entering your mind.

- Maintain physical and mental activities. Exercise has benefits for physical and psychological health (specifically for mood and cognition). There is evidence that regular engagement in mentally challenging and new activities may reduce the risk of dementia. Although we may not be able to exercise together as before, we should maintain physical activities at an individual level. Besides, these personal physical activities can be performed at a group level by setting a common goal, sharing our progress, or creating a friendly competition via social media.

- Pursue outdoor activities while following the guidance of social distancing. Brief outdoor activities are usually still possible and beneficial to health. One can feel much better as a result of sunlight exposure and the ability to see other people while still maintaining physical distancing.

- *Manage cognition, emotion, and mood.* Loneliness is often associated with negative thoughts. Moreover, anxiety and depression may cause social withdrawal which will aggravate the loneliness and isolation associated with social distancing. Conscious breathing, meditation, and other relaxation techniques are helpful for the mind and body and can decrease one's level of anxiety and depression. Emotional support for family members and friends is especially important during this harsh pandemic period, but one should not hesitate to seek help as well.

CHAPTER IV

MITIGATED SPEECH AND POWER DISTANCE INDEX

WHAT IS MITIGATED SPEECH?

Mitigated speech is a linguistic term describing deferential or indirect speech inherent in communication between individuals of the perceived high-power index. Or, in simpler terms, any attempt to downplay or sugarcoat the meaning of what is being said.

Mitigated speech is the act of choosing your words to describe a situation or ask a question in a manner that reduces confrontation or attempts to convey respect, even if it's superficial.

There are usually six degrees of mitigation that makes suggestions to authority:

1. Command – Plan B is going to be implemented.

1. Obligation statement – We need to try Plan B.

3. Suggestion – Why don't we try Plan B?

4. Query – Do you think Plan B would help us in this situation?

5. Preference – Perhaps we should take a look at one of these alternatives.

6. Hint – I wonder if we could run into any roadblocks on our current course.

Or let's try to understand this further with the example of a doctor and patient relationship in a real setting.

Command – "Doctor, I am not going to take the pill. It makes me feel sick."

This involves no mitigated speech. It is the clearest method of conveying a thought or a concern.

Obligation statement — "Doctor, I think I am not going to take that pill. We should consider how it makes me feel."

This is the earliest sign of mitigation in speech. This may be done to soften a statement, possibly to show respect or avoid confrontation.

Suggestion - "Doctor, perhaps I shouldn't take the pill. It might make me sick."

Further mitigated and less to the point.

Query – "Doctor, do you really think I should take that pill?"

At this point, the patient is indicating that the healthcare professional is in charge of the situation but doesn't communicate the concern at all.

Preference - "Doctor, I think it would be better if I took a different pill."

Again, not communicating the real issue and leaving the healthcare professional unsure as to why the patient is considering alternatives.

Hint – "This pill surely looks quite big to swallow."

This has the largest degree of mitigation and is exceedingly unclear regarding the true intent of the patient.

In the US, if a person goes to a store and they like something but find its price to be exorbitant, then they would be direct about their intention by saying, "We can't buy it, because it's too expensive."

Here in India, however, in the exact same situation, we usually tell the shopkeeper *Hum thodi der baad aate hain.* Which translates to "we will come back after some time to purchase it".

We are sugarcoating it and using a form of mitigated speech here, so not to hurt the shopkeepers' sentiments at all.

Being aware of style of speech and level of mitigation can be the first step towards combating confusion in any communication.

Be it for pitching an idea to investors or asking for a raise, mitigated speech is inherent in our communication and is often a turning factor for the desired outcome.

In extreme cases, it can save you from serious chaos.

If you suspect that you employ these mitigation strategies, it may help to practice a different style with the people you engage with every day. You can always seek the assistance of family and friends to observe your speech for mitigation and comment on how you could be more direct.

Culture often plays a significant role in how concerns are communicated and mitigations in speech is used. If this is the factor for you, consider having a close friend or family member advocate for you until you are more comfortable with the idea.

People who communicate more directly can often come across as harsh or too forceful, or even arrogant, to people who prefer mitigated speech. Gladwell explained that because a hint is the most mitigated form of speech, it is *"The hardest kind of request to decode and the easiest to refute."*

People who use a lot of hints often don't communicate clearly to those who speak more directly.

And the problem increases when those who prefer mitigated speech are intimidated by those who use direct speech or when those who prefer mitigated speech really want those who use direct speech to like them and therefore avoid saying anything that might cause a relational tension.

Communication can improve significantly if people can understand the difference between direct and mitigated speech.

Consider marriage, for example. Can you imagine what would happen if a husband and wife grew up in families that communicated very differently. What if, consequently, the husband tends to communicate very directly and the wife indirectly? When two people communicate so differently, they can misunderstand each other which may result in unnecessary frictions in their relationship.

Let's imagine that you've been observing communication for both content and situations, and you're paying attention to when a conversation turns crucial. To catch this important moment, you're looking for signs that safety is at risk.

As safety is violated, you even know to watch for various forms of silence and violence. So, are you now fully armed? Have you seen all there is to see? Actually, no. Perhaps the most difficult thing to watch closely as you're intensely dual-processing is your own behavior. To be honest, most people have trouble distancing themselves from the argument at hand.

Then you've got the problem that other people present when they employ all kinds of tactics. You've got to observe them like an eagle. It is of little wonder then that paying close attention to your own behavior tends to take a back seat. The truth is, we all at times have trouble monitoring our own behavior. We become so consumed with ideas and causes that we lose track of what we're doing along with our sense of social responsibility. We try to bully our way through. We speak when we shouldn't. We withdraw into a punishing silence. We do things that don't work — all in the name of a cause and we invariably find a philosophy to back it.

Unfortunately, when we fail to monitor our own behavior, we can look quite silly. For example: you're talking to your spouse about the fact that he or she left you at the salon for over an hour.

After pointing out that it was a simple misunderstanding, your spouse exclaims, "You don't have to get angry."

And then you utter those famous words, "I'm not angry!"

Of course, you're spraying spit as you shout out your denial and the vein on your forehead has swelled. You, quite naturally, don't see the inconsistency in your response. You're in the middle of the whole thing, and you don't appreciate it one bit when your spouse laughs at you.

You also play this denial game when you ingenuously answer the question, "What's wrong?"

"Nothing's wrong," you whimper.

Then you shuffle your feet, stare at the floor, and look wounded.

What does it take to be able to step out of an argument and watch for the process—including what you yourself are doing and the impact you're having? You have to become a vigilant self-monitor. That means, you have to pay close attention to what you're doing and the impact it's having and then, if necessary, alter your strategy. Watch out, specifically, if you're having a good or bad impact on safety. Control over mitigated speech can be easy if one has control over one's own behavior.

One should only use mitigated speech when chances of someone getting offended are highly probable, as very rarely anything of importance can be said without offending someone.

"He who dares not offend cannot be honest"
Thomas Paine

CHAOS UNDER STRESS

Another factor that impacts mitigated speech is stress, and it can hamper your communication in ways that are unimaginable.

Stress is a big part of everyone's daily life. For example: when you feel overwhelmed with work, when you have too many decisions to make, or when you're caught in a rainstorm without an umbrella while on your way to an important meeting. Stress is experienced as something that's outside of your array of easy management. You can handle stressful situations on some days but on others, because of tiredness or just having too much to do, it can reach such heights that it affects your thinking and communication.

In a way, a stressed-out person can become much too direct in his communication and speak straight to the point out of frustration. This may involve absence of mitigated speech, but the chances of sounding disrespectful and unprofessional also increases. In another scenario, he may wish to keep things to himself and not express them or, if he has to express, he will express it with hints to downplay the message or sugarcoat it completely. In this case, I would say that the primary option is still better off, since in that he is able to express the concern and vent it out of his system; even though the tone or manner in which it's conveyed is not right.

This is what stress does to our communication.

Your communication style changes when you are under stress, which means that the 'right' words don't come to mind easily or you just can't say them without making a conscious effort. Reflecting on how you feel when stressed can become stressful in itself. You may worry that you are not being able to control your feelings, or that you will gain a reputation for being intolerant or impatient, or that people will not want to have you around.

Understanding why you become stressed and how the brain responds to stress may help. Dr. Harry Barry, an Irish author, and medical doctor whose forte lies in mental health, explains the psychological aspects of stress and anxiety in terms of emotions experienced from the flow of information between the 'logical brain' (in the pre-frontal cortex) and the emotional brain or limbic system (in the middle of the brain).

Responses to what we do every day are divided between the emotional and the logical brain. In a panic situation, the emotional brain responds first and you start to feel the normal symptoms of anxiety. If you react to normal anxiety with thoughts of fear and flight, it spirals into panic and you will experience some more symptoms. Before anxiety turns to panic, you must apply the 'logical brain' thinking. If you understand the anxiety and face your fears, the normal feeling of anxiety will run its course without escalating too much and the uncomfortable feelings will subside. The aim is to strengthen the logical brain so that you can control the emotional brain's responses and not allow panic to become overwhelming.

Take for instance the story of Colombian airplane Avianca 52

Which we had discussed earlier.

The National Transportation Safety Board determined that the crash had occurred due to the flight crew failing to properly communicate a fuel emergency. Later on, two NTSB Members filed a dissenting opinion in their report.

Which signifies there are other reasons as well.

Suren Ratwatte, is an accomplished pilot, airline executive, and aviation researcher. He was one of the world's finest Airbus A380 captain, and was also previously Sri Lankan Airline CEO. Suren is a fellow of the Royal Aeronautical Society, a published human factors practitioner in aviation, and also holds a master of aeronautical science specializing in human factors and safety.

His investigation showcased how small problems led to a major one.

- Delayed flight
- Bad weather
- Malfunction of auto pilot
- Long hold patterns
- The plane was old

The plane was old school like we see in movies with many push and pull buttons while current airplanes can be directed using a joystick. Among all the other problems, one of the major issue was that the pilot was operating the instrument with both his hands.

With one hand he was controlling the speed and with the other the instrument. In this situation, he was 'stressed out' with no resources left to do anything else. Decision-making in such a situation falls flat on the face and communication trembles and collapses.

In the black box, the audio recording recovered after the crash, the captain, in the final hours, was heard repeatedly asking for the directions from ATC to be translated into Spanish, whereas all communication with ATS was happening in English.

On many occasions, he asked for the directions to be repeated.

He was so stressed out that he ignored the chance to land the aircraft at the Philadelphia airport which was only six miles away as he was singularly focused on landing at the JFK Airport which was sixteen miles away. Had he had landed at Philadelphia airport he could have avoided the crash. But that's what stress does to us, it makes us do things that we usually won't do in normal stress-free circumstances.

PDI - POWER DISTANCE INDEX

The Power Distance Index is a measurement of the acceptance of a hierarchy of power and wealth by individuals who make up the general population of a nation, culture, or business.

Developed by Dutch social psychologist Geert Hofstede, the PDI ultimately provide insight into the extent to which regular citizens, or subordinates, accept or challenge the authority of a person or people in charge.

Hofstede's PDI is lower in countries and organizations where figures of authority work closely with subordinates, while it is higher in places with a strong hierarchy.

Hofstede's Power Distance Index measures the extent to which the less powerful members of organizations and institutions accept that power is distributed unequally. This represents inequality (more versus less) but is defined from below, not from above.

It suggests that a society's level of inequality is endorsed by the followers as much as by the leaders. For example, Germany has a 35 on the cultural scale of Hofstede's analysis. Compared to the Arab countries where the power distance is very high (80) and Austria where it is very low (11), Germany is somewhat in the middle. Germany does not have a large gap between the wealthy and the poor but has a strong belief in equality for each citizen. Germans have the opportunity to rise in society.

Power Distance Index is one of the major factors which plays a vital role in communication between two parties.

Power Distance is divided into two categories: -

People in societies with a high-Power Distance are more likely to follow a hierarchy where everybody has their own place and doesn't require further justification and high-ranking individuals are respected and looked up to. In societies with a low Power Distance Index, individuals aim to distribute power equally. Without regard to the same level of respect in a high-power distance culture, additional justification is often needed among those in a low-power distance society.

Another parameter that has been added in the table is that of *IDV* which stands for Individualism versus Collectivism. This refers to the strength of the ties that people have with others in their community. A high IDV score indicates weak interpersonal connection among those who are not part of a 'core' family.

It also refers to the strength of the ties that people have to others within their community.

In a collectivist society, however, people are supposed to be loyal to the group to which they belong, and, in exchange, the group will defend their interests. The group itself is normally larger, and people take responsibility for one another's well-being.

Here people take less responsibility for the actions of others and their consequent outcomes.

POWER DISTANCE & IDV NUMBERS

Below are country-wise PDI(Power distance index) & IDV(Individualism) has been mentioned

Malaysia
104 - PDI
26 - IDV
Guatemala
95 - PDI
6 - IDV
Panama
95 - PDI
11 - IDV
Philippines
94 - PDI
32 - IDV
Mexico
81 - PDI
30 - IDV
Venezuela
81 - PDI
12 - IDV
China
80 - PDI
20 - IDV
Egypt
80 - PDI
38 - IDV
Iraq
80 - PDI
38 - IDV
Kuwait
80 - PDI

38 - IDV
Lebanon
80 - PDI
38 - IDV
Libya
80 - PDI
38 - IDV
Saudi Arabia
80 - PDI
38 - IDV
United Arab Emirates
80 - PDI
38 - IDV
Ecuador
78 - PDI
8 - IDV
Indonesia
78 - PDI
14 - IDV
Ghana
77 - PDI
20 - IDV
India
77 - PDI
48 - IDV
Nigeria
77 - PDI
20 - IDV
Sierra Leone
77 - PDI
20 - IDV
Singapore
74 - PDI
20 - IDV
Brazil
69 - PDI
38 - IDV
France

68 - PDI
71 - IDV
Hong Kong
68 - PDI
25 - IDV
Poland
68 - PDI
60 - IDV
Colombia
67 - PDI
13 - IDV
El Salvador
66 - PDI
19 - IDV
Turkey
66 - PDI
37 - IDV
Belgium
65 - PDI
75 - IDV
Ethiopia
64 - PDI
27 - IDV
Kenya
64 - PDI
27 - IDV
Peru
64 - PDI
16 - IDV
Tanzania
64 - PDI
27 - IDV
Thailand
64 - PDI
20 - IDV
Zambia
64 - PDI
27 - IDV

Chile
63 - PDI
23 - IDV
Portugal
63 - PDI
27 - IDV
Uruguay
61 - PDI
36 - IDV
Greece
60 - PDV
35 - IDV
South Korea
60 - PDI
18 - IDV
Iran
58 - PDI
41 - IDV
Taiwan
58 - PDI
17 - IDV
Czech Republic
57 - PDI
58 - IDV
Spain
57 - PDI
51 - IDV
Pakistan
55 - PDI
14 - IDV
Japan
54 - PDI
46 - IDV
Italy
50 - PDI
76 - IDV
Argentina
49 - PDI

46 - IDV
South Africa
49 - PDI
65 - IDV
Hungary
46 - PDI
55 - IDV
Jamaica
45 - PDI
39 - IDV
United States
40 - PDI
91 - IDV
Netherlands
38 - PDI
80 - IDV
Australia
36 - PDI
90 - IDV
Costa Rica
35 - PDI
15 - IDV
Germany
35 - PDI
67 - IDV
United Kingdom
35 - PDI
89 - IDV
Switzerland
34 - PDI
68 - IDV
Finland
33 - PDI
63 - IDV
Norway
31 - PDI
69 - IDV
Sweden

31 - PDI
71 - IDV
Ireland
28 - PDI
70 - IDV
New Zealand
22 - PDI
79 - IDV
Denmark
18 - PDI
74 - IDV
Israel
13 - PDI
54 - IDV
Austria
11 - PDI
55 - IDV
Source - clearlyculture.com

Now let's try to understand this using an example of Indian companies and western country companies.

In Indian companies, we generally use the terms sir/mam when addressing someone who's at a higher position of authority than ourselves. While it is true that western culture has started to catch up with our Indian culture and many Indian companies now have an easy-going and casual working environment where employees can call their superiors by name, the fact remains that the 'sir' and 'mam' culture still prevails to a large extent and it just adds to broaden the communication barrier and levels of mitigated speech in which we sugarcoat our messages a lot more compared to people from the western countries.

In the company where I worked, which was a British MNC, a fresher could call the CEO by his or her name. So, when I started working here, it was pretty difficult for me to convince myself that addressing seniors by their first names is not disrespectful and, for months, I felt a bit uncomfortable every time I did so even though my seniors insisted that I stop calling them 'sir'.

Now, however, I am accustomed to the culture where you are on first-name terms with all your colleagues. I believe that professional relationships can be built in a far better way in an environment where you can look into each other's eyes and communicate freely, rather than the traditional 'master-servant' relationship prevalent at typical Indian offices.

To dwell on this point a little further, let me refer to the times when my parents were working. Back in those days it was unimaginable that someone would call their superior by their name. It was absolutely imperative for them to add the salutations of 'sir' or 'ma'am' even while addressing a person just a rung above them in ranks. Even today, if I have to give the example of government-run banks in India, the culture is still very much deeply rooted in the system to address one another as 'sir' or 'ma'am'.

Let me try to explain this with another example of a night watchman at duty outside your block or building. In India, he would usually greet you with '*SALAAM* SAAB'or*Namaste* and throw a salute at you. However, when I was in London, the security guard in the building where my bother-in-law lived, wore a suit, carried himself stoically and with reserve, and didn't employ the same greeting concept as our security guard does in India.

In India, if you see a security guard doing his duty dressed in a suit then you might have to pinch yourself to make sure you aren't dreaming for, let's face it, we don't have suit wearing suave security guards, do we? It is and has to be a dream. However, on an off-chance that it turns out to be real, then we seldom will appreciate it but most likely demean the person.

Why? Is it because he is less educated?

No! Even highly educated people tend to do the same thing with somebody superior to them. It has little to do with education but more with what you provide as education material here in India. We have had the same education system now for decades. We teach students the Pythagoras Theorem which they would rarely apply in real-life situations but we don't teach them things such as PDI or Mitigated Speech or public speaking, things that would actually come in use in practical life, as aggressively as we teach them, let's say, the method of calculating the velocity of trains.

Now let's talk about the concept of salutation for a minute. In proper English usage, 'Sir' is to be used as a prefix when referring to people who have been Knighted or as a standalone word as a mark of courtesy or respect, but never as a suffix or literal substitute for teacher or senior (unless addressing to the person himself). Understandably, the misuse stems from the attempt to translate Indian conversational honorifics into English.

With India being a strongly hierarchical society, there also exists a taboo in addressing one's superiors with their first names or even as Mr. or Ms. so and so.

In such a situation, and given the absence of similar suffixed honorifics in English, we Indians do *jugaad* with 'sir'.

We, however, have been long out of imperial rule, so let's just start working towards dropping the baggage that they have left behind.

HOW COUNTRIES IMPACT COMMUNICATION

Malaysia is a country that scores high on PDI. Their culture seems to be that where one may not question someone in power like a manager or a government official because authority here is valued. Consequently, the chances of the flow of communication being free and less mitigated are quite dim here.

If I talk about some countries like US or UK, which have moderate power distance and allows a person to question a professor or give ideas to the boss, the communication flows freely as compared to a country like Malaysia. Let's take for example, a British company which has just established its office in Bangladesh and has sent employees from their home country to work there.

A British manager travels to Bangladesh to manage the company and the situation they may encounter might come as a surprise to him.

The British manager may ask a local worker for their opinion on how to do something or improve something and the worker would just sit there still and silent because in his mind he might feel that he doesn't have the authority to speak. Or probably, at the most, would try to give obscure hints rather than directly voicing their opinion.

Egypt is another country that scores high on the Power Distance Index. Students here tend to respect their professors and not question them often, if at all. The country also has exams that determine whether or not a student can continue studying and, by doing this, a level of authority that cannot be surpassed unless done correctly is created.

Students from Egypt, when compared to students in Canada, a country that scores much lower on the Power Distance Index, cannot question a professor on a grade so they may want to have very clear guidelines of what is expected of them in order to succeed.

Students from Canada, for example, are able to question and challenge their professors on why they got a certain grade.

Denmark, as a whole, is considered to be low on PDI.

But what if the culture of a company based out of Denmark or, if I may say, their values or principles don't appreciate their employees raising their voices against the decisions of the managers or supervisors? Though not a direct approach, their actions send the signal to the employees indirectly.

PDI also comes down to the inverse relationship between the code of conduct and the values that the company advocates on their website and how things are at the floor level between a manager and his team.

It also depends on individuals, and how they are able to encourage the flow of information among their subordinates. Is it a free flow or is it restricted to the point where an employee is berated when he asks a question?

Such factors along with many others collectively add to the PDI scale.

For instance, a company operating in Bangladesh goes out to be totally opposite of how they are being measured on a scale of PDI.

They encourage their employees to challenge decisions, they ask their juniors to call them by their name and not acknowledge them by 'sir' or 'mam'.

No matter which country you live in and whether it has low PDI or high PDI, it's important to raise your voice for what is right and communicate it in a way that the impact of your message doesn't lose its meaning.

Be clear in your communication, avoid mitigated speech, and speak freely and confidently. These can be managed and done effectively by a small act of inculcating such things into your brain. When you are aware of these things, it becomes easier for you to manage difficult situations and circumstances.

Malala Yousufzai comes from Pakistan, a country with a high PDI.

In fact, PDI is at such a high level in Pakistan that some states have banned girls from attending school. But Malala Yousufzai was particularly inspired by her father's work and was educated in a way that such constriction couldn't pull her back from what she wanted out of life.

In early 2009, when she was 11 or 12, she wrote a blog under a pseudonym for BBC Urdu, detailing her life during the Tehrik-I-Taliban's Pakistan occupation of her district, Swat.

The following summer, journalist Adam E Ellick made a New York Times documentary about her life as the Pakistan military intervened in the region. She rose in prominence giving interviews in print and television and was nominated for the international children's peace prize by activist Desmond Tutu. On 9th October 2012, while on a bus in Swat district, after giving an exam, Malala and two other girls were shot by Tehrik-I-Taliban gunmen in retaliation for her activism.

After recovering from the attempted assassination, Malala became a prominent activist for Right to Education being vocal about what she believed in and what was right.

The PDI of a country is not impacted by the name of the country itself but by its people, their education, belief, and conditioning. All of these factors lead to impacting the PDI of a particular country.

Being static in our approach can bring frustrations and trouble. One can always learn though by looking into history for examples of people who were able to break stereotypes and achieved excellence by not constricting themselves by how things had been running in their society and the way it was fabricated to provide an individual a safer future, but not the knowledge of how to embrace a less explored territory. One should have a flexible approach rather than a static approach that believes in labeling itself with only one thing or two things for an entire lifetime.

Take for example these two personalities, which will better illustrate this point.

Rabindranath Tagore and Amartya Sen were both bestowed with Nobel Prizes for their extraordinary work in their respective fields — literature economics. Both of them also share a connection.

Amartya Sen was more inclined towards creativity over the traditional competitive exam mindset of the stereotypical educational system.

In the year 1990, an essay published a factual story that exposed one of the most atrocious crimes to have been ever reported in India. It exposed the fact that the Indian population census was missing around 3.7 crore women, and that Sonography machines were being used by doctors to diagnose the sex of unborn children.

The story shook the entire country and paved the way for a strict law to be passed against female feticide.

This story of the missing women was brought to people's attention by none other than Amartya Sen. Sen's contribution to society ranges from welfare economics, social choice theory, social justice, and decision theory the to economic theory of famines.

He began his schooling at St Gregory's School in Dhaka in 1940. The next year he was admitted to Patha Bhavan, Shanti Niketan, where he completed his school education. In this school, there was no room for people interested to get their children into competitive exams. It stressed on cultural diversity and embraced cultural influences from the rest of the world.

The founder wanted his school to be:

"...the connecting thread between India and the world. A world center for the study of humanity somewhere beyond the limits of nation and geography."

Amartya Sen felt fortunate enough to be a student in this institution which brought in the mix of the West and the East.

The institution taught him not to limit himself to any one discipline, one view of the world, or one belief, but to explore its width as much as possible.

The school's founder was none other than the poet, philosopher, and the first Nobel laureate of India, Rabindranath Tagore. It was also Tagore who had given Amartya Sen his name.

Unfortunately, our conditioning today misses this point and is happy in the safe havens of things already tried and tested that ensure safe passage through life without taking the pain of wandering into less tread territories and exploring new lands.

Rabindranath Tagore also gave the title of 'Mahatma' to Mohandas Gandhi and had written the national anthem of two countries, namely India and Bangladesh. Tagore hated formal education and spent his early years reading subjects such as anatomy, mathematics, and even Sanskrit.

Although he was sent to the UK by his father to become a barrister, he indulged himself in studying Shakespeare and other English writing and eventually returned to India without actually obtaining any degree.

Tagore hated trapping a child inside a classroom for, according to him, the human mind inside four walls was far away from the beauty of nature and hence his classrooms were in the open under the shade of trees.

Amartya Sen's strong support for gender equality was due to the education imparted in this institution.

Amartya Sen's mother was a judo student and learned the sport in the 1920s when it was quite unusual, a taboo even, for women in India to tread such waters. Even to this day it is unimaginable for the majority of the population as their beliefs are quite fixed on the matter that women are best suited for household works.

The wide array of things in which Sen has contributed in is the result of his conditioning and schooling which happened in Rabindranath Tagore's institution. A multicultural and stress-free environment led Sen to choose the subject of his own interest, and he was free to choose the books that interested him without any restriction.

This freedom allowed him to read stories from all around the world. He read the writings of George Bernard Shaw and the stories of Leo Tolstoy introduced him to the concepts of social justice, parity, and liberty.

The freedom and conditioning to explore and pursue an eclectic brand of education and not restraining his mind to a fixed belief is what brought Amartya Sen his Nobel Prize.

I am not against formal education but I believe a certain amount of width is required in our approach in deciding what is best for a child, as the formative years play a vital role in determining their future.

Rabindranath Tagore's believes were in contrast to practices prevalent almost a century ago and though things have changed a lot since then and the education system has improved quite a bit, a lot of ground still needs to be covered for further improvements. To change a country's face, one needs to start thinking about a child from their primitive years and educate not only the child but one's self as well in a wide array of fields to figure out what the best is.

CHAPTER V

SILENCE

"The World suffers a lot not because of the violence of bad people, but because of the silence of good people"
Napoleon Bonaparte

WHY DO WE CHOOSE TO STAY SILENT WHEN WE WITNESS SOMETHING WRONG?

To understand whether the policies of a company is in practice, employees must be willing to communicate suspected wrongdoing (whistleblowing).

But it cannot be assumed that the employees who see or suspect any wrongdoing will actually say something. It has been estimated that less than half of all employees who witness wrongdoing report it.

This is not a case of bad communication, but totally the lack of it.

We all like to believe that we are highly moral people and when faced with a hard choice we will do the correct thing. But the evidence suggests otherwise. Good people often find themselves in situations that make strong social cues or even overt pressures to withhold information about misconduct.

Friedrich Nietzsche was a German philosopher who was able to explain the paradox of morality more than a century ago and which still holds itself true in parts. It has been well described in Nietzsche explanation how ethics develop and the consequences one may face for a master type living in a world that's dominated by the morality of a slave. Nietzsche argued that there are two explanations for how morality develops. One part of the story is bio-psychological, in terms of what morality resonates with what psychological type of person someone is. The other part of the story is cultural, because different moral codes develop under different survival circumstances. Nietzsche searched through history for the survival circumstances that necessitated the development of slave morality and found its roots in the Judeo-Christian tradition, in a critical set of events that occurred early in Jewish history — the enslavement of Jews in Egypt. The significant result of the Jews being enslaved for a long time was the development and internalization of the moral code suitable for surviving slavery. Suppose you are a slave; how do you survive? And if you have children who are born into slavery, what survival strategies will you teach them? In order to survive, a slave must obey the master, and this does not come naturally. So, the first lesson is: you must stifle your nature.

Suppose the master strikes you, the desire for revenge comes naturally, but you have to stifle it. Suppose the master tells you to wait, being inactive does not come naturally to you, but you must suppress your desire for activity. Suppose the master tells you to do something you don't want to do, something that is morally wrong and may cause physical or psychological injury to another, then also you must override your desire to do what you want and obey. In short, you must train yourself to restrain your natural impulses and to internalize a humble, patient, obedient self. You know you must do this because slaves do not want to end up dead. Things may not be at such an extreme in the current professional environment, but one cannot deny that it bears no resemblance to it. Even prisons have been modernized and are better than they were before, but they still are prisons.

Consequently, Nietzsche asserts that slave virtues have survival value. Obedience, humility, forgiveness, and patience are essential for slaves and these are the traits that they will drill into their children if they want them to survive; and so over time, the slave virtues become cultural values. Such values make them strongly resent the master but they eventually believe that silence is better and resentment kept suppressed within is safer than exploding with it on the master and hurting their own selves. Silence in most parts where such unjust things occur has been enveloped as cultural values. People who choose to remain silent have found a philosophy to back it and, sadly, they pass it on to others in their social circle. Parents pass this over to their children, friends within their group, teachers to their students, etc.

Very few are actually able to express their resentments and take the corrective action of speaking up and the majority of people use silence or, I would say, the highest form of mitigated speech to express their dissatisfaction, which in turn has next to no chances of making any impact or correcting any wrongdoing.

Evidence suggests that silence is a problem in both the public and private sectors and in large as well as small organizations. No matter how much some companies advocate free communication in their policies, the ground report is quite different.

Speaking up has its own benefits.

An employee at the Gurgaon-based subsidiary of a multinational company wrote to the head office alleging that some vendors here were companies managed by the Indian arm's CEO through his relatives. The parent company hired Hill & Associates, a risk audit firm, to investigate. The allegations turned out to be correct: the vendor companies were run by the CEO's relatives, and he got a part of their profits.

This entire episode and the illegal use of power came to light only because the employee chose to speak up or, in this case, write to the head office.

According to a study in Harvard business review, several executives' finest moments came when they gathered the courage and confidently expressed disagreements with their bosses and peers. To their surprise, they found out that they were treated with more respect after these episodes. Doing the right thing is a reward in itself both in the short-run as well as in the long professional run.

One should be taught that every rewarding career will invariably bring its shares of ups and downs, bad days, bad weeks and bad months. Everyone faces setbacks and has to navigate through discouraging desperate situations at some point or the other in their lives. Some people abandon their plan when they hit these bumps. They lose their way and ultimately challenge their own performance and the wound they receive feels all the more painful because of it being self-inflicted. While others take the challenge head-on and wade their way through the obstacles until they achieve their goals.

There is nothing anyone can do to prevent you from reaching your potential. The challenge is for you to identify your dream, develop the communication skills to get there, and exhibit character, grit, and perseverance. Then once you reach your milestone, you need to have the courage to periodically, reassess, make alterations, and pursue a course that echoes who you truly are.

"Courage isn't having the strength to go on – It's going on when you don't have strength"

NAPOLEON BONAPARTE

People are often afraid to communicate in team meetings, whether they are one-to-one or conference/board meetings. Even though people have the intelligence within them to contribute to these meetings, they refrain from communicating their thoughts because they fear that they lack the knowledge or the courage r whatever it might be to speak up and communicate clearly.

Many great ideas die because they aren't communicated correctly. To be honest, agreeing is usually easier than confronting someone, at least in the short run. And it feels good when someone nods at something we say or acknowledge.

Disagreements though are an unavoidable, normal, and strong part of relating to other people. There is no such thing as a conflict-free work environment or a conflict-free life. You might dream of working in a peaceful paradise, but it wouldn't be good for your company, your work, or you. It is, at best, an utopian dream that has little relevance in reality. In fact, disagreements, when managed well, can have a lot of positive results.

An article in HBR by Amy Gallo points out some benefits of the approach.

Better work outcomes: When you and your coworkers push one another to continually ask if there's a better approach to a certain situation, that creative friction is likely to lead to new solutions.

"Conflict allows the team to come to terms with difficult situations, to synthesize diverse perspectives, and to make sure solutions are well thought-out," says Liane Davey, cofounder of 3COze Inc. and author of *You First: Inspire Your Team to Grow Up, Get Along, and Get Stuff Done.*

"Conflict is uncomfortable, but it is the source of true innovation, and also a critical process in identifying and mitigating risks."

And there's rarely a fixed amount of value to be gained in a disagreement. If you and your colleague are arguing about the best way to roll out a new initiative — he wants to launch in a single market first and you want to enter several at one time — you'll be forced to explore the pros and cons of each approach and ideally find the best solution.

Opportunities to learn and grow: As uncomfortable as it may feel when someone challenges your ideas, it's an opportunity to learn. By listening to and incorporating feedback, you gain experience, try new things, and evolve as a manager; because good communication is not only about speaking but also listening. When a peer chews you out after an important presentation because you didn't give her team credit for their work, the words may sting, but you're more likely to think through everyone's perspectives before preparing your next talk.

Improved relationships: By working through conflict together, you'll feel closer to the people around you and gain a better understanding of what matters to them and how they prefer to work. You'll also set an important precedent - that it's possible to have "good" fights and then move on.

Higher job satisfaction: When you're not afraid to constructively disagree about issues at work and communicate the conflict confidently, you're likely to be happier to go to the office, be satisfied with what you accomplish, and enjoy interactions with your colleagues.

Instead of feeling as if you have to walk on eggshells, you can focus on getting your work done.

Research supports this. A study of American and Chinese employees in China showed a correlation between the use of certain approaches to conflict management — one in which employees pursue a win-win situation, care for others, and focus on common interests — and an employee's happiness at work.

A more inclusive work environment: If you want to have diversity and inclusion in your organization, you have to be prepared to disagree in communication.

Anesa Parker, Carmen Medina, and Elizabeth Schill wrote in their Rotman Management article, "Diversity's New Fronteir: Diversity of Thought", that "While homogenous groups are more confident in their performance, diverse groups are often more successful in completing tasks."

They went on to explain that managers and employees need to get over an "instinctual urge to avoid conflict" and drop "the idea that consensus is an end in and of itself.

In a well-run diverse team, substantive disagreements do not need to become personal. Ideas either have merit and posits of connection or they do not.

•

ACADEMIC SCORES ARE NOT YOUR COMMUNICATION SCORES

You may be good at certain things and it may land you a job at a good company that picks employees based on certain skills. But once you are in, what differentiates you from another person who is working there is whether they possess the same set of skills as you do.

Just for an example, and this is a personal one from my post-graduate college. A campus placement was going on for the postgraduate students. There were only two rounds — group discussion and personal interviews — and, trust me, there were people who scored extremely well in their exams but were not able to crack the GD.

There were also people who were just the opposite and who scored poorly in the exams but were able to crack the GD because their communication skill was way better than the others. People with high academic scores choose to stay silent in group discussions or maybe they lack the skill to speak in front of an audience. For some, such skills come naturally while others have to learn it. You may get a job with your qualification but how you move forward depends largely on your communication skills and, some part of it, on your technical expertise and how the company envelopes its message.

Many organizations portray the message, verbally or non-verbally, that falling in line is the safest way to hold on to our jobs and our careers. They may be having the best of friendly policies for an employee's welfare, but how it is practiced and whether or not it is put into action at all is that matters the most.

The Speak-Up policy of a company with over 10,000 employees just had 70 cases of speak-ups in a year when, on the other hand, the discussion over coffee is all about the wrong things happening by everysecond person. The need for quiet submission is exaggerated by today's difficult economy, where millions have lost their jobs and many more are at the edge of losing it.

Sometimes, people who speak up get their day in the sun. Edward Snowden is a prime example of that. It is believed that he has earned more than $1.2m in speaking fees since he leaked confidential US material to various outlets and went into exile later in Moscow.

Snowden has also released a book called Permanent Record and a movie was made on him titled 'Snowden' where his character was played by Joseph Gordon Levitt.

But sadly, public recognition of a few doesn't mean that speaking out is necessarily viewed as courageous and praiseworthy.

Most individuals who go against their organization or express their concerns publicly are severely punished indirectly. If they are not fired outright, they are usually marginalized and made to feel irrelevant.

There are companies whose values are such that they encourage speaking out but whether those values are practiced becomes a subjective point. Many times, and often with the best of intentions, people decide that it is more productive to remain silent about their differences than to air them. But as new research shows, silence doesn't smooth things over or make people more productive. It merely pushes the difference beneath the surface and can set in motion powerfully negative forces. When people stay silent about important disagreements, they can begin to get filled with anxiety, anger, and resentment. As long as the conflict is unresolved, their blocked feelings remain strong, making them increasingly distrustful and all the more fearful that if they speak up, they will be embarrassed or rejected. Their sense of insecurity grows, leading to further acts of silence.

These brutal moments of silence can be replaced with righteous spirals of effective communication, but that requires individuals to find the courage to act differently and officials to create the kind of environment in which people will value the expression of differences.

In the end, whether our primary concern is to preserve our relationship or to get our tasks done as expeditiously as possible, we must speak up rather than withhold our difference. Otherwise, we risk undermining both our relationships and our ability to complete our work.

WHEN TO ZIP YOUR MOUTH

Even when a difference is addressed, there is always the question of timing. It may be fruitless, for example, to raise a difficult issue with your partner when you see a frown on their face. There are no hard and fast rules about what needs to be discussed or when it's best to do so. You must rely on your best judgment for that depending on the kind of situation you are in. What is important is that you shift your mindset from asking yourself whether this is one of those rare times when you should speak up to asking whether this is one of those rare times when you should remain quiet?

Depending upon your own answer, you'll have to slowly and steadily work toward your problem. For example, if you always have chosen to stay silent, start by speaking for 10 to 15 seconds about a continuing discussion and then when your confidence improves, speak for some more time.

But be mindful of situations when it is better to stay silent, for there are a few instances when you should just Zip-it!

If you have to give a lecture or speech and the microphone isn't working or the lights aren't effective, and yet you try to continue anyway? Don't be that guy. Call off the Talk. Reschedule it or find another way to get everyone the information afterward.

Sometimes your remarks won't work. You can tell when you're losing an audience (provided you pay attention). So, if you can't get their attention back, the ideal move usually is to find a way to wrap things up.

When you ask a question, you should wait for the answer. Otherwise, it seems that the only reason you asked was to provide an additional chance for you to talk. It becomes rhetorical. Granted, sometimes that might be intentional, but if it's not, show a little restraint. Be quiet and listen.

At times, the best way to achieve more is by saying nothing. Maybe, instigated by your silence, people will say things they otherwise wouldn't have. Psychiatrists are masters at it and they know exactly how to obtain what's on their patient's minds by asking questions gently and then holding themselves back and allowing the patients to speak freely.

Silence can be used as a tactic too. For example, suppose you're in a negotiation and the other side basically revises its position in your favor without you even saying anything.

Don't make it easy for them. Let them give into the awkwardness and speak first.

Sometimes people have important things to say and sometimes they simply need someone to hear them out. Be a good listener in these circumstances, and keep quiet so that others can have their say when they need to.

It is also imperative to stay silent or choose your words carefully when you are angry or annoyed. We all have moments when we know we're going to say something that we'll regret and yet we can't stop ourselves from saying it. It's better, in these kinds of situations, to avoid speaking altogether.

Most people appreciate good advice. However, there's no easier way to make yourself look and sound unprofessional than to seize every opportunity to show how much you know.

When you have to resolve conflict - I'm not saying to always be silent to avoid conflict since some conflicts are helpful and it can help both parties grow and improve. However, not all arguments can help both parties grow and, oftentimes, there are trivial arguments that can come up. If your friends try to tag you into some argument or debate you don't want to be in, then just telling them point blank that you're not interested will be a better option.

When in group conversations, especially if you're not familiar with those you're talking with, it is often a better idea to be silent and to watch and learn from those who are around you. Unless you choose to pitch into the conversation by adding your own viewpoint or pointing out something that has been omitted or is helpful, you must sit back and watch for the first few moments after you have introduced yourself and enter the conversation at a later point when you have something in your mind that can connect the dots in the ongoing conversation.

While some people say you ought to be more outgoing and talk more, I would, quite on the contrary, suggest that it is better to watch and reflect on yourself before you become more outgoing and talk more.

Of course, there isn't a hard and fast rule to follow this approach. You can always be outgoing and try your hand at communicating with people and make adjustments in due course by learning from the weak points that hold you back at such moments. Reflecting upon yourself and learning from experiences can boost the conversation and you will be able to add your own points to it a lot better and more logically if you've got some time to observe first. You'll appear more affable and build rapport faster if you understand who you're talking with and what you're talking about.

One thing that there is to understand is that you also don't want to remain silent and observe for too long, as there are chances that the group will perceive you as weird and unsettling. Always make sure to pitch in every now and then.

SILENCE AT WORKPLACE

An article by Sujaya Banerjee, which was published in the Times of India on 26th November 2021, better explains the point of why people choose to keep themselves silent at the workplace; and adds to the other views which were shared previously on the same topic.

You ask your team a question about a recurring problem during an online meeting, but no one responds. You call for an in-person meeting with the team to kick-start a new intervention that can revolutionize how you do business with your customer. Everyone takes copious amounts of notes while you speak for thirty minutes straight but then you stop to ask: Any questions? Do you think this will work? What else must we do to make this possible? There is complete silence.

If this is a situation that you commonly encounter, then your team may be lacking the psychological safety to speak up.

These times of upheaval have not only accelerated change, learning, and innovation, but have also yanked many organizations out of their industrial-era mindsets and compelled them to adapt to the knowledge-era cultures, where creative ideas and employee voice become key to solving difficult problems.

If you're leading a team that's now remote, its physical and psychological safety should be a priority for you. Most organizations are doing a good job of applying social distancing and other measures to protect their members physically. But what about their psychological safety? An employee who feels psychologically safe feels included, free to learn and contribute, and challenges the status quo without fear of being embarrassed, marginalized, or punished if they speak up with candor. People flourish when they participate in a cooperative system with high psychological safety that covers three basic human needs — fulfillment, belonging, and security.

That's what makes it so powerful when present, and also so dangerous when absent. Psychological safety makes people confident of speaking up and even sharing mistakes without fear of punishment or negative consequences. It's a sense of permission for being forthright and can allow access to mission-critical information or market intelligence, or an opportunity to learn from mistakes, by enabling the comfort to share this. Psychologically safe workplaces are not about being nice or being free from conflict, where everyone agrees with each other, or where all ideas will be accepted. They are instead healthy places of fearless speaking up, with accountability to solve problems, so that teams can make the most optimal decisions.

Psychological safety is not an outcome in itself but a process leading to a goal — excellence, that comes from:

a) Timely employee voice.

b) Encouraging alternative perspectives and deliberate divergence of thought and listening.

c) Sharpening the creative problem-solving process that triggers innovative ideas/ solutions.

However, this is how it looks when teams lack psychological safety:

*Employees don't ask many questions during meetings.

*They don't own up to mistakes and instead place blame on others when mistakes are made. There are, consequently, missed opportunities for lessons learned.

* The team avoids difficult conversations & hot-button topics lest these lead to conflict.

* Feedback is not given and neither sought.

* Senior executives and team leaders mostly dominate discussions and meetings.

* Employees hesitate to ask each other for help lest it displays their vulnerability.

* Employees mostly don't know each other personally, and keep a safe distance from one another.

* There are hardly any differing points of view or disagreements.

Does all this sound familiar? Remote working appears to have accentuated these behaviors in some teams, and if this resonates with you, then your team lacks psychological safety.

Let's then look at what can you do to improve this situation that adversely impacts engagement, voluntary contribution, and performance:

Listen. Show your team that you're engaged:

a) If your employees feel that you don't pay attention when they speak, or that you don't value their thoughts and opinions, they'll shut down.

b) Demonstrate engagement by being present during meetings. This includes active listening by making eye contact, nodding, and summarizing what the team members are saying.

c) Ask questions to make sure you understand the other person's ideas or opinions. By actively engaging, you create an environment where people feel it's not only OK to speak up, but it's encouraged and accepted.

Avoid blaming to build trust:

It's easy when something goes wrong to look for someone to blame. But to build and maintain psychological safety in the workplace, focus on solutions.

Instead of "What happened?" and "Why?" ask "How can we make sure this goes better next time?" Notice here the focus on the collaborative language.

"We" statements turn the responsibility into a group effort, rather than singling out an individual for a mistake.

Bring your whole self to work and create self-awareness for team members:

People should bring their whole self to work — their unique personalities, preferences, and work styles.

Build self-awareness in your team by sharing how you work best, how you like to communicate, and how you like to be recognized. Encourage team members to do the same.

Toxic energies & cliques must be nipped in the bud:

If team members speak negatively about their peers, talk to them about it. Be clear and let them know that you work together as a team and negativity will not be tolerated.

Any kind of groupism, bullying, and marginalizing of any individual or group must be nipped in the bud.

Include your team in decision-making:

Consult your team when making decisions. Ask for their inputs, thoughts, and feedback. Not only will this help them feel included in the decision-making process, but will also build psychological safety and lead to more positive outcomes.

Once a decision is made by you, explain the reasoning behind it. How did their feedback factor into the decision? What other considerations were made? Even if your employees don't agree, they'll appreciate the honesty and transparency behind how the decision was made.

Encourage practice through feedback:

When employees feel psychologically safe, they feel empowered to give feedback — up, down, and across. And this means they feel comfortable in approaching the leader when there's critical information to share.

Invite your team to challenge your perspectives and push back. While this may be uncomfortable at first, healthy conflict within teams leads to better decisions and greater accountability, making it a win-win for all. You might also want to lead by example by taking interpersonal risks and sharing failures.

Role-modeling growth mindsets are key to setting off the virtuous cycle of learning.

Try getting up at the next all-company meeting and share a failure story, and what you learned from it.

Be the coach & champion development of teams:

Let the team know you're on their side by supporting their personal and professional developments.

Find the time for this. Share the team's work with senior leadership to increase visibility of what your team is doing — and give credit to team members when it's due.

Why building psychological safety pays off?

It's the means to excellence, as proven by various research studies. It is the number one driver of high performance.

Attempting to build psychological safety, especially in challenging times, in the workplace is key to enhancing the employee experience.

The writer is the CEO of Capstone People Consulting.

DEPART FROM THE ACCEPTED STANDARDS BY ACTING DEVIANTLY

To break down the walls of silence, we sometimes have to behave in ways that are not considered suitable for a particular organization.

According to American Psychological Association, lack of clarity in communication makes it hard to follow and difficult for the listener to share a common focus of attention and meaning with the speaker. Communication deviance is thought to be a long-term attribute within families that may engender inefficient patterns of thinking and information processing. It is also thought to be associated with schizophrenia and other psychological disorders.

Put differently, we must act deviantly.

For example, we can choose to ask tough questions in a meeting where employees just accept the decisions of the top management. Although deviance often carries certain negative meanings with it, it is not identical to dysfunctionality. Deviance is, at heart, an imaginative act – a way of searching out and inventing new approaches to doing things.

Émile Durkheim, a French sociologist, believed that deviance is a necessary part of a successful society and that it serves three functions:

1) It clarifies norms and increases conformity.

2) It strengthens social bonds among the people reacting to the deviant.

3) It can help lead to positive social change and challenge people's present views.

By challenging a particular norm, we can play a role in changing it.

Deviance can also encourage the dominant society to consider alternative norms and values.

Rosa Parks' act of deviance in Montgomery, Alabama, in 1955 led to the U.S. Supreme Court's declaration that segregation in public transportation was unconstitutional.

Rosa McCauley was born in Tuskegee, Alabama, in 1913. When she was two years old, her parents separated. Rosa moved with her mother to Pine Level, Alabama, to live with her grandparents. Rosa's mother taught at a school in another town and was able to come home to see her children only on weekends.

Rosa missed her mother, but she loved being with her grandparents. She learned how to plant corn and milk cows from her grandfather and her grandmother taught her how to cook and make quilts.

Rosa's grandparents also taught her about racism. In the American South, laws kept black people separate from white people. Black people had to use separate entrances, drink from separate fountains, and go to separate schools and hospitals. They were also often attacked by groups of white men. The whites would set fire to black homes, churches, and schools. Rosa's grandfather had to board up the family's windows so no one could break-in. From a very young age Rosa learned to be brave.

In 1955, she was arrested for sitting on a bus. As in many cities in the South, the buses in Montgomery, Alabama, were segregated. Black people had to sit at the back. If a white person wanted to sit, a black person had to give up his or her seat. On December 1, Rosa refused to get up. She was arrested. Many claimed Rosa was just tired. But she was a member of the National Association for the Advancement of Colored People (NAACP) and it was a deliberate protest from her side, it was an act of defiance.

BUILD A COALITION

Reaching out to others can give us the strength to break the hold of silence. Not only is it easier to speak up when we know we are not alone, but a coalition also carries more legitimacy and resources.

Even though it may feel threatening at first to approach someone to join forces with you, it may actually be a surprise by how often you will find that many people feel the same way as you do.

That's what happened to Nancy Hopkins, a scientist at MIT

Hopkins repeatedly found herself having to fight harder than her male colleagues even for a basic resource like lab space. After dealing with one issue or the other for years, she finally drafted a letter to the MIT administration.

Before sending it, however, she showed it to a female colleague who she regarded to be politically savvy. To her surprise, the other woman wanted to add her signature to the letter as well, for the same type of things had happened to her too. In the end, fourteen out of the fifteen women Hopkins approached decided to sign on it. It is only through a coalition that work unions make their messages stronger.

India's first-ever non-congress government is also an example of a coalition.

Since India's independence, the Indian National Congress ruled the nation.

The first Prime Minister Jawaharlal Nehru, the second PM Lal Bahadur Shastri, and the third PM Indira Gandhi were all from the Congress party.

However, Raj Narain, who had unsuccessfully contested the election against Indira from the constituency of Rae Bareilly in 1971, lodged a case against her alleging electoral malpractices. In June 1975, Indira Gandhi was found guilty and barred by the High Court from holding any public office for six years.

In response to this verdict, an ungracious Emergency was declared under the pretext of national security.

The next election's result was that India's first-ever coalition government was formed at the national level, headed by The Janata Party, under Prime Minister Morarji Desai, which was also the first non-Congress national government, that existed from 24 March 1977 to 15 July 1979.

Before building a coalition, you should be aware of its advantages and disadvantages.

Kenna Knight, Professor at University of Kentucky, in her article, *UKNOWLEDGE,* has listed some advantages and disadvantages of forming a coalition:

There are many advantages to joining or forming a coalition. There are also several disadvantages.

Both the advantages and disadvantages may be immediate or long-term, direct or indirect.

It is important that organizations understand that the benefits will generally outweigh the costs of collaborating.

The most common advantages are:

• Improved communication on issues
  • Potential for professional development
  • Elimination of duplication
  • More readily available resources
  • Improved public image and communication
  • Better needs assessment

Some common disadvantages are:

  • Slower decision making
  • Turf protection or lack of trust in other organizations or members
  • Some limitation to resources
  • Unequal commitment from organization members

• Possible lack of focus on the primary issue

• Difficulty finding time to meet

• Not having the right organization representative at the table who can commit to the group and make decisions

Before beginning the process of joining or forming a coalition, carefully consider all the pros and cons of it. Also keep in mind that coalitions are a lot of work, and be sure to fully understand what is expected of you as a member of the coalition.

CHAPTER VI

HOW ASSUMPTIONS AFFECT COMMUNICATION

THE PROBLEM WITH ASSUMPTIONS

Many barriers in communication branch out from wrong assumptions.

Wrong assumptions are generally made because the sender or the receiver does not have the requisite knowledge about each other's backgrounds.

Imagine you are in office and you see your boss passing by at a distance. He also sees you and you wave an enthusiastic 'hi'. But he doesn't stop, doesn't respond, and you start wondering why you are being ignored.

The boss is data and him not saying 'hi' to you in return is your interpretation of it. But now, he may be running to the washroom and he doesn't want to stop for anyone.

Think of a situation where you have learned in the past the traits of body language and are confident about your intellect that you will figure out if a person is speaking the truth or not.

Trust me, you can be very wrong. It might turn out to be just your assumption and not the truth. And if you don't trust me, then you have to trust Chris Voss.

Christopher "Chris" Voss is an American businessman, author, and academic. Voss is a former FBI hostage negotiator, the CEO of The Black Swan Group Ltd, and co-author of the #1 best-selling book *Never Split the Difference.*

He is an Assistant professor at Harvard Law School and Georgetown University's McDonough School of Business, and a lecturer at the Marshall School of Business at the University of Sothern California.

In his book, he says that usually, we see one criminal and one hostage. But in reality, things can be a bit different. Voss mentions that with time things have evolved. He says that in such type of situations, nobody works alone. In one of his standoffs with a criminal, he said that "We had as many as five people on the line, analyzing information as it came in, offering behind-the-scenes input, and guiding each other through their separate inputs." Some would argue that you really need a whole team to understand one person. The fact is that it is not really that easy to understand someone's intention whilst communicating.

We are easily distracted and most of the time our listening is quite selective, hearing only what we want to hear, and the rest we just assume or interpret ourselves with our arsenal of data. Imagine a scenario where you are running a restaurant or a hotel and you have a group of boys aged between twenty and thirty as guests. They are young and carefree and prove to be a bunch of troublemakers with their actions disturbing the other guests in the hotel. So, you as the owner, ask them to leave and decide that in the future you won't allow such a group in your establishment again.

What has happened in this scenario is that one instance involving one particular group of young boys has led you to assume in your mind that every such group that will come into your hotel will create a similar mess and therefore you have decided to restrict the entry of such groups.

You have created a fixed filter or, I would say, a lens in which you judge all of them on one single scale.

Something similar happened back in the year 2015, in Kasol, Himachal Pradesh. Kasol is a small village in Himachal Pradesh and is a popular tourist destination for Indians and foreigners alike for its picturesque sceneries and natural beauty. It is also known as mini-Israel as most hotels, restaurants, and the local banners and boards, are in Hebrew and almost all locals can speak the language. It is also common to see Israelis roaming the streets.

An Indian woman was allegedly not allowed to order food in an Israeli café by the name Free Kasol, and some say that she was not even given the menu. According to a post shared on Facebook by Stephen Kaye, the owner of the café, an Indian descent herself, refused to give the woman a menu claiming that it was a 'Members only' café. However, when Stephen Kaye, a foreigner, asked for the menu, he was promptly given one.

When, in an interview, the owner was asked about the whole fiasco, two different stories popped out of it. One was that there was a misunderstanding. It was said that the waiter handed the menu to the friend who accompanied the girl, as they only give one menu to a table occupied by two people, and that was the reason the girl, an Indian national, was not given the menu, but her foreign national friend was.

The other side of the story that came out was the owner's bitter past experience with a few guests of Indian nationality who had come to the café under the influence of alcohol and had created a ruckus.

That was one of the reasons that they had to filter the guest coming to their café. But the menu and other things written over there are in Hebrew, which only Israelis, or people trained in it, can understand.

There are many sides to this story, and one side is starkly relatable in which we make assumptions out of a situation and then act accordingly in the future and avoid such things in the first place even if there is no sign of it occurring again. Developing such assumptions closes the window of connection through which we could learn so many things from others. One should always have an open mind when it comes to interacting with people. There will be instances when a few gestures of someone would remind you of a bitter experience you had in the past, but assuming how the current event might shape out based on past experiences may not be a wise thing to do.

Malcolm Gladwell in his latest book, *Talking to Strangers*, examines Communication between strangers and why they often go awry. Looking at moments in history—Fidel Castro fooling the CIA, the trial of Amanda Knox in Italy, the death of Sandra Bland—Gladwell points out flaws in people's perceptions of one another and how they draw those conclusions.

His thought-provoking prose weaves through the psychology of human tendencies and the consequences of our mistaken judgements and incapability to understand the strangers around us.

In an interview Gladwell mentions about a real-life story of a CIA spy whom he addressed by the name of *The Mountain Climber,* and who,according to him, was kind of the Michael Jordan of the CIA.

He talked about how everyone worshipped The Mountain Climber. When The Mountain Climber was in Eastern Europe, the Soviets used to have courses for their young KGB officers in training that were modelled on him, and about what it means and what it takes to be a great spy.

He ran the CIA's Cuba espionage operation out of Havana; and was a great favorite among the Cubans. Gladwell mentioned that The Soviets were able to track down The Mountain Climber and, offering him suitcases full of cash, said, "If you just come and work with us, this is all yours. We'll give you millions of dollars in cash." To which he refused.

He spoke many languages, and always like a native. His tradecraft was impeccable. He was the spy's spy, and he made James Bond look like a bungler.

But here comes the part which made this top CIA operative look like a fool or, should I say, an amateur in his craft.

Gladwell introduced the character of Florentino Aspillaga in the interview, you can find that in the book as well.

Florentino was someone high up in the Cuban intelligence service who was transferred to run Cuba's intelligence operations in Czechoslovakia during the Cold War in the 1980s. But he decided to defect, because he'd grown disillusioned with Fidel Castro, and he crossed the border with his girlfriend in the trunk of his Mazda and showing up at the U.S. embassy in Vienna, he said, "My name is Florentino, Aspillaga. I'm a senior official in the Cuban Intelligence Directive. I have a story to tell."

He specifically asked for the Mountain Climber.

He then got to sit with him and began narrating his story.

The first thing that The Mountain Climber said to him was, "Tell me your story." And Florentino said, "El alpinista..." (Spanish for mountain climber), "When you were in Havana running the serious operations, you were my hero. I worshiped you. I followed your every move. I wanted you to be present when I told you this story. You ran a ring of spies when you were in Havana, didn't you?"

"Yes, of course I did, The Mountain Climber said," And Florentino said, "Well, you know, this one guy you had who you met in such a place and he worked for this government and told you the following secrets..." And the mountain climber exclaimed, "Yes!" And Florentino said, "That guy was working for us. He was a double agent."

It was a devastating piece of revelation for The Mountain Climber.

And then Florentino said, "I'm not done. You know, the other guy who worked for this agency and gave you the following secrets? He was working for us too."

The Mountain Climber felt like he was literally having the worst day of his life.

And then Aspillaga said, "Oh, I'm not done yet. You know this other spy, you had to work with to boost your defense intelligence? He was working for us as well."

And the mountain climber had lost his capacity for speech. He spoke in shock. But Florentino was not done. He then proceeded to name forty-eight spies — the entire network of spies that the mountain climber was running in Havana during his years there — and revealed that every single one of them was a double agent working for Fidel Castro the whole time.

The greatest field operative of his generation had been fooled not once, not twice, but 48 times over the course of many years.

Now, this is a super interesting story for a number of reasons.

"The Mountain Climber is as good as it gets. Yet he still got deceived" - Malcolm Gladwell.

A small country like Cuba with a limited budget working relatively crudely. Rather, it's something that happens to even the best of us who are highly skilled at what we do. Right? And that even the best of us who are highly skilled at what we do can be deceived over and over again for many years without realizing that we're being deceived in that way. And that, according to Gladwell, is an extraordinarily important fact in trying to understand how the world works. I am sure we can all relate to this story.

There are, at times, situations when our experience falls flat and our hardbound assumptions for someone are proved wrong time and time again. The capacity for being wrong in our assumptions is something that lies within all of us. According to Gladwell, one of the tasks we have as human beings is to learn how to adapt to our fundamental gullibility. Most people approach an argument by their pre-conceived thoughts or with their assumptions that they pour out in words.

One such argument occurred between farmers and the National Oil Company of Iraq when Saddam Hussein was ousted by a 2003 U.S.-Led invasion.

Oil had been discovered in Basra, 420 km southeast of Baghdad, and a letter was drafted to the farmers to vacate the fields for digging oil. The farmers were naturally displeased and were willing to go to any extent to save their fields. Oil, which is considered to be the backbone of Iraq's economy, was left in tatters after years of war and economic sanctions. Baghdad signed a series of deals with oil companies to develop its vast oil reserves that could boost its output potential to Saudi Arabian levels and generate billions that were needed to rebuild the country.

It is even said that the National Oil Company threatened to bring in the army to clear the fields from farmers. The farmers on the other hand were willing to fight till death for their land.

A massive bloodshed was about to begin but was averted by a very last-minute intervention when the oil ministry set up a committee to negotiate with the local communities. They played the role of negotiator instead of the one played by the previous government of a commander, giving order and threats to the locals.

They asked the farmers, "How long will it be before you expect to produce oil on this?"

The farmers said, "Probably three years."

Another inquiry from the negotiator was about the plan the farmers had in mind of what do in the land over the next few months. The negotiator then asked the farmers about the challenge of vacating the fields.

Their main concern was the harvest, which was due in six weeks; and which represented everything they owned. Shortly thereafter, an agreement was reached. The farmers could harvest the crops and they would not impede the activities of the oil company. Indeed, the oil company hoped to hire many of the farmers as laborers for construction activities.

And they did not object if they continued to plant crops in between oil derricks. This is how the bloodshed was averted peacefully and without employing any force but just by a simple method of listening and understanding.

A question then subsequently arises — how do you overcome communication assumptions? Here are 3 ways to challenge your assumptions:

- Ask questions rather than assuming. Instead of basing your decisions on what you think you know, ask questions to get more information and clarification.

- Response In, React Out. Much of our lives are spent in reacting to others and to events around us. The problem is that these reactions may not always be the best course of action and, as a result, they can make others unhappy, and make things worse for us.

Why would we want to make things worse?

Leo Babauta, a blogger at Zen Habits, explains it this way:

The truth is, that we often react without thinking. It's a gut reaction, mostly based on fear and insecurities, and it's not the most rational or appropriate way to act.

Responding, on the other hand, is taking the situation in, and deciding the best course of action based on values such as reason, compassion, cooperation, etc.

Let's take a quick example:

React:

Your child breaks something. You immediately react by getting angry, perhaps yelling, upsetting the child and yourself, worsening your relationship, and not making anything better.

Respond:

Your child breaks something. First: you notice your angry reaction, but pause, take a breath, and consider the situation. The first response is to see if your child is OK — are they hurt, scared, etc.

Second: realize that the object that is broken, in the larger view, is not that important. Let it go, adjust to a world without it.

Third: help her clean up, make a game of it, and show them that mistakes happen and that it's not something to dwell on.

Fourth: calmly talk about how to avoid mistakes like that in the future and give them a hug.

Make a habit of seeing the positive in everything. I know it's easier said than done, but things become easy when we practice this habit. Ask for clarification if you need it; and if you want to assume something, then assume that the person has a positive or neutral intention and isn't purposely trying to hurt you.

Even if you have evidence that the person in question is acting negatively intentionally, understand that this has much more to do with them than with you. Don't take it personally.

People also ask, what are the barriers to the communication process?

Communication barriers are factors that hamper the effectiveness of communication.

They result in a disparity of understanding of the message between the sender and the receiver. These barriers can occur at any stage of the communication process—sending, encoding, transmitting, decoding or receiving. Whenever two people are together, there's communication. Interpersonal communication includes not only verbal communication, but also non-verbal communication. For example, what *do* those raised eyebrows mean? Why is she making faces? Why is he staring! The recipient of the communication, whether verbal or non-verbal, interprets the potential meaning of that particular communication. Someone raising their eyebrows frequently in a conversation can be seen as a sign of surprise for some while for others it may be a sign of doubt or disbelief or exaggeration. We all interpret things differently and that is because of our conditioning and past experiences. Barriers to interpersonal communication occur when the sender's message is received differently from how it was intended and yes, that can be because of the sender not being able to articulate his point clearly or it can be because how we are perceiving it. Typically, communication breakdowns result from a lack of understanding without clarification and the best way to tackle such problems is to ask questions. If barriers to interpersonal communication are not acknowledged and addressed, the harvest of a conversation can suffer.

Language Differences

Interpersonal communication can become twisted when the sender and the receiver of the message speak different languages. Not everyone in the workplace will understand slang, jargon, acronyms, etc.

Instead of seeking clarification and asking questions to clarify the doubt, people might employ guesswork to fathom the meaning of the message and then settle on mistaken assumptions. Also, misunderstandings may occur among people who do not speak the same primary language. As a result, feelings may be hurt due solely to the misconceptions of words or of body language.

An example can be: A professor of linguistics goes to an engineering college to deliver a lecture on Aeronautical technology. The professor uses subject-specific words that are extremely technical and intricate for a layman. In such a case, the students are likely to lose attention and curiosity in the topic

The best way to tackle it is to understand that you should communicate in a common language that everyone understands easily. Avoid complex words to make an impression of being an intellectual. Even if you use some technical terms, make sure you are breaking it down to the simplest of forms for your audience.

Remember the scene from 3 Idiots where the professor asks his students a question, "what is a machine?" and asks the curious Amir Khan, who was smiling at him, to tell the definition of a machine.

He answers, "A machine is anything that reduces human effort."

That is how simple it should be. But no, some people have the innate personality of making things complicated or making them look intellectual. As in that scene, as the professor asks him to elaborate it further, he tries to do that by giving examples of day-today things such as if you are feeling cold you can switch on the heater and make yourself comfortable, and that's a machine. If you're feeling hot you can turn on the fan, and that's a machine. The telephone too is a machine, and a few other simple examples.

But the professor was reluctant to hear the definition of the machine and called him an idiot. And then asked someone else for the definition.

A frontbencher raised his hand and answered the definition "Sir, machines are any combination of bodies so connected that their relative motions are constrained and by which means, force and motions may be transmitted and modified as a screw and its nut, or a lever arranged to turn about a fulcrum or a pulley about its pivot, etc. Especially, a construction more or less complex consisting of a combination of moving parts, or simple mechanical elements as wheels, levers, cam, etc."

Both explained it correctly but which one was easier to understand?

I am sure the readers of this book and the viewers of that movie were able to decide on that without an effort.

Cultural Differences

Interpersonal communication can be hampered by a lack of cultural understanding, misperception, bias, and stereotypical beliefs. Workers from a certain workplace may have limited skills or inexperience in communicating with people from different backgrounds.

Many companies offer a range of training to help employees understand how to communicate more effectively across cultures and relate to those who may have different background experiences. Similarly, gender barriers can hinder interpersonal communication if men and women are treated differently, and held to different standards, causing interpersonal conflicts at the workplace.

People from different backgrounds communicate differently depending on how they have been conditioned or raised. For example, Europeans tend to indulge in a high level of eye contact and most often are direct in their communication. They use less of mitigated speech and are easy with rejecting requests and saying no. People from Asian cultures, on the other hand, may see direct eye contact while conversing as unapproachable or rude and use indirect communication or mitigated speech to be polite, providing hints instead of being to the point.

Generational Differences

Interpersonal communication can be complicated by generational differences in speech, dress, values, priorities, and preferences. For instance, there may be a generational divide as to how team members prefer to communicate with one another. If the younger workers remain cooped up in cubicles and use social networking as their primary channel of communication, then it can alienate them from the older workers who may prefer face-to-face communication. Broad generalizations and stereotypes can also cause interpersonal rifts when a worker from one generation feels superior to those who are younger or older. Biases against workers based on age can constitute a form of discrimination.

The only way to eradicate assumptions out of your communication is to be aware about such barriers.

HOW INTENTIONS PLAY A PART

Intentions strongly influence our judgments of others. If someone intended to hurt us, we judge them more harshly than if they hurt us by mistake. We're willing to be troubled by someone if they have a good reason, and we're annoyed if we think they just don't care about the bearing of their actions on us.

The Battle Over Intentions

Consider the story of Kabir and Ananya, who have been in a relationship for two years and get into frequent fights which are painful to both of them.

The couple was at a party thrown by some of their common friends, and Ananya was about to reach for another scoop of ice cream, when Kabir said, "Ananaya, why don't you put off the ice cream?" Ananya, who struggles with her weight, gave Kabir an aggressive look, and the two avoided each other for a while. Later that evening things went from bad to worse:

Ananya: I really disliked the way you treated me in front of our friends at the party.

Kabir: The way I treated you? What are you talking about?

Ananya: About the ice-cream. You act like you're my father or something. You have this need to control me or put me down.

Kabir: Ananya, I wasn't trying to hurt you. You said you were on a diet, and I'm just trying to help you stick to it. Why are you so defensive? You hear everything as a direct outburst on you, even when I'm trying to help.

Ananya: Help? Humiliating me in front of my friends is your idea of helping? Shouting at me in front of your friend is what you call help?

Kabir: You know, I just can't win with you. If I say something, you think I'm trying to embarrass you, and if I don't, you ask me why I let you eat that dessert or take that extra drink. I am sick of this thing. Sometimes I believe that you start these fights on purpose.

This conversation left both Ananya and Kabir feeling angry, hurt, and misunderstood. What's worse, it's a kind of situation they encounter over and over again. They are engaged in a battle over intentions: Ananya accuses Kabir of hurting her on purpose, and Kabir denies it. They are caught in a cycle they don't understand and don't know how to break.

There is a way out though. Two vital mistakes in this conversation make it significantly more difficult than it needs to be — one by Ananya and one by Kabir. When Ananya says "You have this need to control me or put me down," she is talking about Kabir's intentions.

Her mistake is to assume that she knows what Kabir's intentions are, when in fact, she doesn't. It's an easy mistake to make. And most of us do it all the time in the real world.

Kabir's mistake is to assume that once he clarifies that his intentions were good, Ananya is no longer right in being upset. He explains that he "wasn't trying to hurt" Ananya, that in fact, he was trying to help her.

And having explained this, he thinks that it should be the end of it. As a result, he doesn't take the time to learn what Ananya is really feeling or why. This mistake, too, is common.

Fortunately, with some awareness, both these mistakes can be avoided.

The First Mistake: Our Assumptions About Intentions Are Often Wrong

Exploring "Ananya's mistake" requires us to understand how our minds work when constructing stories about what others' intentions are. And in turn, we should learn to know the set of uncertain assumptions upon which these stories are built.

Here's the problem: While we care deeply about other people's intentions toward us, we don't actually know what their intentions are. We just can't. Other people's intentions exist only in their hearts and minds. They are invisible to us. No matter how real and right our assumptions about other people's intentions may seem to us, they are often incorrect.

Much of the first mistake can be traced to one basic error: we make an attribution about another person's intentions based on the impact of their actions on us. We feel hurt, and therefore think that they intended to hurt us. We feel insulted, and therefore think that they intended to insult us. Our thinking is so automatic that we aren't even consciously aware that our conclusion is only an assumption.

We are so taken in by our own story and conditioning of what they intended that we can't imagine how they could have intended anything else.

The conclusions we draw about intentions based on the impact of others' actions on us are rarely true.

When a friend shows up late to the movie, we don't think, 'I bet he ran into someone in need.' It's more likely that we think, 'What a jerk, always comes late on purpose.'

When we've been hurt by someone else's behavior, we assume the worst for everyone. Lakshmi fell into this outline. She had her shoulder operated on by a prominent surgeon, a man she found to be bad-tempered and hard to talk to. When Lakshmi hopped in for her first appointment after surgery, the receptionist told her that the doctor had unexpectedly extended his vacation.

Irritated, Lakshmi assumed her wealthy doctor enjoying himself on the beaches of Pondicherry with his wife or girlfriend, too thoughtless and irresponsible to return on schedule. The picture of it in her mind intensified her anger.

When Lakshmi finally saw the doctor a week later, she asked him rather rudely how his vacation had been. He responded that it had been wonderful. "I'll bet," she said, wondering whether to raise her concerns.

But the doctor went on, "It was a working vacation. I was helping set up a hospital in Chennai. The conditions there are just horrendous."

Learning what the doctor was really doing didn't erase the inconvenience Lakshmi had endured. Yet knowing that he was not acting out of selfishness but from an unrelated and generous motivation, left Lakshmi feeling substantially less bitter about having to wait the extra week.

We attribute intentions to others all the time. In business or in office, work is often conducted via e-mails, voicemails, faxes, and conference calls, and we have to read between the lines to figure out what people really mean.

When a customer writes: "I don't suppose you've gotten to my order yet" is he being cynical? Is he angry? Or is he trying to tell you that he knows you're busy? Without the tone of voice to guide us, it is easy to assume the worst.

We often tend to treat ourselves more generously than others, and what's ironic — and all too human — about our tendency to attribute bad intentions to others is how differently we treat ourselves. When your husband forgets to pick up the dry cleaning, he's irresponsible; but when you forget to book the movie tickets, it's because you're overworked and stressed out.

When a coworker criticizes your work in front of colleagues, she is trying to put you down; but when you offer suggestions to others in the same meeting, you are trying to be helpful.

This is because when we're the ones acting, we know that most of the time we don't intend to annoy, offend, or upstage others. We're wrapped up in our own worries and are often unaware that we're having any negative impact on others. When we're the ones acted upon, however, our perception easily slides into one about bad intentions and bad character.

Are There Never Bad Intentions? Of course, there are! Sometimes we get hurt because someone has meant to hurt us. The person we are dealing with is horrible, selfish, or sadistic, and they are out to make others look bad on purpose.

But these situations are rarer than we imagine; and without hearing the other person's side of the story, we can't really know their intentions.

Getting intentions wrong can be costly, intentions matter, and guessing wrong can be hazardous to your relationships. We assume bad intentions means bad person. Perhaps the biggest danger in assuming that the other person had bad intentions is that we easily jump from "They had bad intentions" to "They are a bad person." We settle into judgments about their character that cements our views of them and, indeed, affect not only any conversation we might have but the entire relationship.

Once we think we have someone figured out, we see all of their actions through that lens; and even if we don't share our views with them, the impact remains. The worse our view of the other person's character, the easier it is to justify avoiding them or saying nasty things about them behind their backs. When you find yourself thinking "That traffic cop is a control freak" or "My boss is controlling" or "My neighbor is unbearable," ask yourself why your view is this? It might have been just one instance that didn't go well that has caused you to perceive them in that way, but is it fair to mold your entire view on that person with that kind of negativity just because of that one instance?

Accusing others of bad Intentions creates defensiveness. Our assumptions about other people's intentions can also have a substantial impact on our conversations.

The easiest and most common way of expressing these assumptions is to ask these critical questions: Why did you want to hurt me?

Why do you ignore me like this?

What have I done that makes you feel that it's okay to step all over me?

We might think that we are sharing our hurt, frustration, anger, or confusion; but we are actually trying to begin a conversation that will end in greater understanding between you and another person, perhaps some improved behavior, and maybe an apology.

What they might think we are doing is trying to provoke, accuse, or malign them (in other words, they make the same mistaken leap in judging our intentions) and given how frequently our assumptions are incomplete or wrong, the other person might feel not just accused, but falsely accused. There's hardly anything more aggravating than that.

We should not be surprised, then, that they will try to defend themselves or retaliate. From their point of view, they are defending themselves from false accusations. From your point of view, they are being defensive. The end result is a mess.

No one learns anything, no one apologizes, and nothing changes.

Ananya and Kabir fall right into this category. Kabir is defensive throughout and at the end, when he says that he sometimes wonders if Ananya "starts these fights on purpose", he actually accuses Ananya of bad intentions; and thus begins the cycle of allegations.

If asked about their conversation afterwards, both Ananya and Kabir would report that they were the prey of the other's bad intentions. They both would claim that their statements were right.

Our assumptions about the other person's intentions often come true, even when they aren't true to begin with. You think your boss isn't giving you enough responsibility, and you assume that this is because they don't trust you, or your ability, to do the work well.

You feel demotivated by this, and figure that no matter what you do, it'll not change your boss's mind. Your work suffers, and your boss, who hadn't been concerned about your work before, is now worried and critical of you. So, they end up giving you even less responsibility than before.

When we think that others have evil intentions toward us, it affects our own behavior. And how we behave, in turn, affects how they treat us.

THE INNER FILTERS

Without even realizing it, we tend to cover up our feelings by using communication filters which can present itself in the form of words, body language, and actions.

When your best friend asks, "What's wrong?" and you instinctively smile and say, "Nothing," you might be closing yourself off from your actual feelings. Shutting the door to your inner world in this way prevents you from fully experiencing life, connecting with your personal values, and making choices that help you live in sync with them.

Don't beat yourself up though if you use filters as an emotional technique, for you just might be practicing a form of self-care. Filters can serve as an important defensive mechanism in case of shock or difficult-to-cope-with emotions to a particular situation. In these scenarios, you might require a temporary filter on your feelings.

Turning on or activating the fullest expression of your emotions when you are not ready can re-trigger unpleasant or even traumatic experiences. This can be counterproductive to a healing process, which is necessary in order to have an internally active life.

That is not to say that you have to be fully healed and at peace in all moments or be cheery every day to have an internally active life. Filters can often distort your true feelings and hinder the relationships you have with yourself and others in the form of communication, which gets awry during such situations. Subconscious filters contaminate how you communicate your feelings. You pick up these filters for a variety of very understandable reasons like the fear of not being good enough or the fear of being hurt.

But filters end up diminishing the message you're trying to get across and affect communication in both directions.

External filters

When we first meet someone, our brain begins to instantly process information about what we see, hear, and feel about them.

To understand what I mean, think of a person you care about. When you do, you'll notice an overflow of emotions and memories. To listen well is to understand that much of our present experiences don't come from our present, but from our memories and our past experiences. And often it is not even a memory of the person we're talking to right then, but of someone different and from long ago. We react from warehoused responses, not new reactions.

These are the filters through which we all listen. We hear everyone through our own filters of memories, desires, perceptions, and biases. These filters are limited, even irrational, in the sense that they cannot respond in a new way to what is happening, because we are busy responding to something in the disconnected past. Our brains are wired to make unconscious judgments about the behavior of others so that we can move through the world without spending much time or effort in understanding everything that we see.

Understanding is hard as it requires deep thinking, patience, compassion, and an open mind.

"Thinking is difficult, that's why most people judge." ~ Carl Jung

Human behavior specialist, Dr. John Demartini, refers to this phenomenon as "self-righteous" and "self-wrongous."

Judging is simply our attempt to create a hierarchy of better than and lesser than, superior to and inferior to, and to attach worth to everyone and everything that we meet.

We have an innate urge to be right, to be better, to be superior. Our view of the world around us necessitates us to be either right or wrong, and so we tend to judge.

Here are two theories in psychology that explain the phenomenon of judging:

Attribution Theory

"It's not whether you win or lose, it's how you place the blame." ~ Oscar Wilde

Gestalt psychologist Fritz Heider is often described as the "father of attribution theory." Attribution is a term used in psychology that deals with how individuals view the causes of everyday experiences as being either external or internal. Models to explain this process are called attribution theory. Psychological research into attribution began with the work of Fritz Heider in the early 20th century, and the theory was further advanced by Harold Kelley and Bernard Weiner.

In his 1920's dissertation, Heider addressed the problem of phenomenology: why do perceivers attribute properties such as color to perceived objects, when those properties are mental constructs? Heider's answer was that perceivers attribute that which they "directly" sense – vibrations in the air, for instance – to an object they construe as causing those to sense data. "Perceivers faced with sensory data thus see the perceptual object as 'out there' because they attribute the sensory data to their underlying causes in the world." Heider extended this idea to attributions about people — "motives, intentions, and sentiments, the core processes which manifest themselves in evident behavior.

Humans are inclined to allocate causes to their actions and behaviors. In social psychology, attribution is the process by which individuals explain the causes of behavior and events. Attributions are thoughts we have about others that help us make sense of why people do the things that they do. More often, our focus is on the behavior, and we ignore the situation or the framework or the circumstances which lead to that behavior.

There are two types of attribution:

External

External attribution, also called situational attribution, refers to interpreting someone's behavior as being caused by the individual's environment. For example, if someone's car tire is punctured, it may be attributed to a hole in the road. By making attributions to the poor condition of the road, one can make sense of the event without any issues that it may, in reality, have been the result of their own bad driving. Individuals are more likely to associate unfortunate events with external factors than with internal factors.

Example: A child attributes his feelings to the weather outside his house; he feels sad because it is raining outside, or irritated because it's too hot outside.

Internal

Internal attribution, or dispositional attribution, refers to the process of assigning the cause of behavior to some internal characteristic, likeability, and motivation, rather than to outside forces. In this case, individuals feel that they are personally responsible for everything that happens to them.

Example: Contradictory to the example given for external attribution, a child attributes the weather to his feelings; it is raining outside his house because he is feeling sad. Or his friend is upset and is not responding to calls because two days ago he didn't get back to him after he had called. Someone died and that's why it's thundering or raining outside because of some connection of the elements with the deceased.

Another important factor explained under the attribution theory is cultural bias.

Culture bias is when someone makes an assumption about the behavior of another person based on their own cultural practices and beliefs. An example of cultural bias is the separation of "individualistic" and "collectivistic cultures". People in individualist cultures, like in North America, Germany, Ireland and Australia, value individualism, personal goals, and independence.

People in collectivist cultures are thought to regard individuals as members of groups such as families, tribes, work units, nations, and they tend to value conventionality and interdependence. In other words, working together and being involved as a group is more common in cultures that view each person as part of a larger community.

This cultural trait is common in Asia, traditional Native American societies, and Africa.

Research shows that culture, be it individualist or collectivist, affects how people make attributions.

People from individualist cultures are more inclined to make fundamental attribution errors than people from collectivist cultures. Individualist cultures tend to attribute a person's behavior to their internal factors whereas collectivist cultures tend to attribute a person's behavior to external factors.

Research suggests that individualist cultures engage in self-serving bias more than collectivist cultures, i.e., individualist cultures tend to attribute success to internal factors and failure to external factors. In contrast, collectivist cultures engage in the opposite of self-serving bias, or self-effacing bias, which is: attributing success to external factors and blaming failure on internal factors (the individual).

Projection (Seeing Our Darkness in Others)

"Knowing your own darkness is the best method for dealing with the darkness in other people." ~ *Carl Jung*

As Swiss psychiatrist, Carl Jung said, "Although our conscious minds are avoiding our own flaws, they still want to deal with them on a deeper level, so we magnify those flaws in others."

We can only see in others what we have inside ourselves. First, we reject, then we project.

Jung stated our shadow to be the unknown, unconscious, dark side of our personality. According to Jung, the shadow— being instinctive and irrational— is prone to psychological projection in which perceived personal inferiority is recognized as a perceived moral deficiency in someone else.

American-British psychologist Raymond Cattell, known for his psychometric research, identified 16 factors or dimensions of personality that we all possess.

All of our personalities are actually made up of the same traits, and we differ only in the degree to which each trait is expressed.

According to Cattell, people simply express these traits in different ways, at different times, and in different areas of their lives. Some may be dominant, and some may be dormant.

When we judge someone for something, we are actually judging ourselves for the very same thing; it's just that we haven't fully owned or accepted that trait yet within us.

So, when we judge, does it reflect upon others or ourselves?

"When you judge others, you do not define them, you define yourself." ~ *Earl Nightingale*

The world around us is our mirror, and judging someone does not define who they are but who we are.

More often than not, the things we detest and judge in others are a reflection of the things we cannot accept about ourselves.

The yardstick we use for ourselves is the yardstick we use for the world. The way you measure yourself is how you measure others, and how you assume others measure you.

"If you hate a person, you hate something in him that is part of yourself. What isn't part of ourselves doesn't disturb us." ~ *Hermann Hesse*

Everything that annoys us about others can lead us to an understanding of ourselves.

Judging is relative, and is our continual comparison or validation of everything that we perceive with what we believe. Our beliefs may be a function of our own personality traits, our conditioning (at multiple levels like societal, cultural, or religious), and our life experiences.

Judging shuts us down and prevents us from understanding the full situation or a truth that is not known yet.

"Through judging, we separate. Through understanding, we grow" ~ Doe Zantamata

While judging, one gets stuck in a loop; but you can break the loop and change by consciously trying to escape that circle. Here are a few ways to do that:

Be Open - Before we judge, let us try to understand things with an open mind. Being open-minded means having the skill to consider other viewpoints and being empathetic to other people, even when you disagree with them. One needs to have enough courage to have their ideas challenged or, I would say, to encourage people in a positive way by challenging their ideas.

Be Curious- We can remain curious by acknowledging the fact that there might something about a particular situation that we may not fully understand. We need to listen without judgment and ask questions relentlessly.

Be Empathetic- Let us be empathetic and give the benefit of doubt to others for their condition or circumstances that may not be in our full understanding. Research has shown that empathy makes people better human beings in all areas of their lives. They become better at relations with their family members, friends, and colleagues .

Be Self-Aware- Practice being self-aware through self-forgiveness, self-acceptance, and self-compassion. You can probably go back to the chapter about self-awareness and consider reading it again.

The more we understand ourselves, the more we can understand others. Knowing our own inclinations will help us assess others fairly, patiently, and compassionately. It's unwise to say, "Stop judging others," as it is not as straightforward as it seems and all our attempts against our innate human nature may go in vain. It is similar to telling an individual to stop thinking about something that is bothering him, which, frankly, is a stupid advice to give as it is impossible to stop our thinking process. We should instead advise him to focus his attention on something else. We can also learn to become more self-aware when we judge and, through that awareness, move on to adopt more interesting thought patterns.

We can also be more grateful and compassionate of the world around us for what it is, rather than trying to fit it into our eyes.

"Be kind. For everyone you meet is fighting a battle you know nothing about." ~ Ian MacLaren

There is an acronym we can use when the urge of judging someone kicks in.

GGNE

Gender- It is not because of how they are dressed, it's because we're biological creatures of different sexes, the first thing we notice on meeting another person is which gender the person is.

Generation or age - Are they children or are they adults Are they wise? Are they dependent?

Nationality or ethnicity – What color, creed, or type of person they are.

Education level — As we talk to them or as we see how they are dressed, we will draw some conclusions about their educational level, which is sort of socioeconomic.

Emotions – After taking in and processing these other details, we would sort of be fantasizing about their emotions or what they might be feeling.

This process of making judgments is incredibly fast. In fact, it is so fast that we are no longer open to receiving any real or original information from people.

We are just stuck in the efficiency of generalization. Personal experiences and our conditioning distinguish how we view the world and how we communicate. One person may see the world through his own set of filters and another person would see it through a different one.

The more similar people are in lifestyle, experience, culture, and language, the more similar their mental filters would be.

People who come from very different social and economic backgrounds must work hard on themselves to exactly communicate what's on their minds.

SO HOW DOES GENIUSES HANDLE IT?

"Be curious, not judgmental." – Walt Whitman

"I am grateful that I am not as judgmental as all those censorious, self-righteous people around me." – Anonymous

Although people who have achieved mastery at understanding and connecting with others also have these filters, they understand and are aware of how their brain works. When they notice that they are getting stereotypes or generalized impressions, they set these filters aside.

They open themselves to another person instead of being self-concerned, and manage to turn down their inner noise and focus on the other person.

Let me tell you an interesting little story.

A man was waiting at an airport for a long-distance flight. His flight was delayed and so he had a little spare time. One could tell that he was a rich man since he was wearing a Tom Ford suit and had a Louis Vuitton bag with him. He saw some cookies in a cafeteria shelf and thought that he should treat himself. He bought quite a few cookies because he thought that it might be a quite long delay. He then took a seat beside a man who was in a casual worn-out attire and had a shabby look on his face but with a beaming smile plastered to it.

The man in the suit started to read a magazine he had picked up earlier. He exchanged a glance with the other man and then tried to avoid eye contact as he went back to reading. While he was engrossed in his magazine, he happened to see that the man sitting beside him boldly grabbed a cookie from the container he had bought. He initially ignored the incident to avoid a scene and grabbing a cookie himself, went back to his magazine. But the man seemed to have enjoyed the cookie so much that he took another one and started eating that too. This continued for a while and with each passing moment, the man in the suit began to get more and more irritated.

Every time he took a cookie, so did the other man. When there was finally only one cookie left, the shabby man nervously took it and breaking it in half, offered it to the suited man with a smile. He took the cookie and could not believe the other man's nerve. He was thinking in his head how audacious and ungrateful that man was?

The other man then got up and left and while going, he took the container with him. This suited man couldn't believe what had just happened. He was relieved when his flight was called, and he began gathered his belonging. But as he lifted his bag; he saw that there was a full container of cookies right there — the one he had purchased. He was totally shocked. He realized that the cookies he had been eating actually belonged to the shabby man. He felt embarrassed and ashamed in his heart that while he was angry and irritated, the other man was being generous and kind. He felt terrible about it and searched for the other man to apologize to him, but he couldn't find him anywhere.

So, what does this story tell us? It tells us that things are not always as they appear.

If we want to be really good with other people, we first need to renovate ourselves so that we don't let our decisions, opinions, or beliefs take our consideration away from another person. If we don't have peace of mind, if we are not comfortable with ourselves, if we are feeling the slightest bit insecure, then guess what happens? the other person begins to feel insecure too.

For this, try using the method that I have been using after reading about it in an article by Leo Babauta.

It's the DUAL method.

Here's what it is:

Don't pass judgment. If you find yourself being judgmental, stop yourself. This takes a greater awareness than we usually have, so the first step (and an important one) is to observe your thoughts for a few days and try to notice when you're being judgmental. This can be a difficult step, so remind yourself to observe.

Once you're more aware, you can then stop yourself when you feel that you're getting judgmental. Then move to the next step.

Understand. Instead of judging someone for what he's done or how he looks, try instead to understand that person. Put yourself in their shoes. Try to imagine their background. Talk to them, if possible. Find out their backstory, for everyone has one. If not then try to imagine the circumstances that might have led the person to act or look the way they do.

Accept. Once you begin to understand, or at least think that you kind of understand, try to accept. Accept a person for who he is, without trying to change him. Accept that he will act the way he does. The world is what it is and, no matter how hard you try, it will continue to remain what it is long after you're gone. Accept that, because otherwise, you'll be in a world of frustration.

Love. Once you've accepted someone for who he is, try to love him. Even if you don't know him, even if you've hated him in the past, love him as a brother, or love her as a sister. No matter who they are, old or young, light-skinned or dark, male or female, rich or poor, love them.

What good will loving someone do? Your love will likely only be limited, but it could have an effect on two people: yourself, and possibly the person you've found love for.

Loving others will serve to make you happier, trust me on this one. And it will also change the lives of others, if you choose to express the love and take action on it.

ASSUMPTION THAT WE MAKE OR SELF IMAGE THAT WE HAVE CREATED

A self-image of yourself that stops you from speaking in front of people.

Once there was a teacher who didn't want to talk in public. But because he was a teacher, he had to and so, to avoid feeling his fear of public speaking, he used to read out from his notes and rarely gave presentations where he would speak without reading his notes.

This self-image that he had created for himself was a result of something that had happened to him back in school when he was giving a presentation. His mother was also there and although he had thought that he did well, he later discovered that his mother was very embarrassed for him; and she made it a point to bring this to his attention.

Though his mother's intention was probably to make him do better in his next presentation, but the shock of her embarrassment went into his experience and a part of his brain said, 'Boy, I'm never going to do this again.'

So, for decades he carried this inhibition about talking out loud in front of a group.

Don't you think the same happens to us?

Our first bad experience of tasting a dish stays with us forever and we don't eat anything related to it. On our first interaction with a stranger, we may find them to be rude and we perceive that every stranger would be the same, and we don't try walking up to a new person at a meeting or in a social gathering, as we keep thinking about our past experience.

"It's not who you are that holds you back, it's who you think you're not"
-Anonymous

Some people hesitate to stand in front of an audience and speak because they have experienced bitter humiliation at school or some other place during some point of their lives. And they assume that the same thing is going to happen at every stage of their life and as a result, choose to remain quiet so to avoid facing the same humiliation again.

Assumptions kills desire.

Most of the times assumptions stop us from communicating. Don Miguel, in his book The Four Agreements, have clearly described how making assumption impacts our communication.

He writes:

'We have the tendency to make assumptions about everything, and the problem with making an assumption is that we believe they are the truth, we could swear they are real. We make assumptions about what others are doing or thinking – we take it personally. Then we blame them and react by sending emotional poison with our word. That is why whenever we make assumptions, we are asking for problems. We make an assumption, we misunderstand, we take it personally, and we end up creating a whole big drama for nothing.

We make assumptions and believe that we are right about the assumptions we have made. Then we defend our assumptions and try to prove someone else wrong. It is always better to ask questions than to make assumptions, because assumptions set us up for suffering.

Further in the book, it is clarified by a real-life example:

You decide to get married and you make the assumption that your partner sees marriage in the same way that you do. Then you live together and you find out that is not true. This creates a lot of conflicts but you still don't try to clarify your feelings about marriage.

The husband comes home from work and the wife is upset and the husband doesn't know why. Maybe it's because the wife made assumptions without communicating with him as to what she wants, as if he can read her mind, and got upset when her expectations were not met. Making assumptions in a relationship leads to a lot of fights, difficulties, and misunderstandings between two people.

HOW OUR LIMITING BELIEFS AFFECTS OUR COMMUNICATION

What Are Limiting Beliefs?

Have you ever made a statement like, "I'm not good at math" or "I have a heavy voice and would never make a good singer?" These are examples of limiting beliefs that are put in the center of your mind and, in turn, you allow such beliefs to define you. Such beliefs are mostly set at a very early stage in life and shockingly many people live on such beliefs till there last breath. Because of the way our brain develops, we are emotionally more susceptible to the experiences that we have early on in life than the ones we have later in life. Limiting beliefs are the lies that our brain tries to tell us. It is a state of mind, conviction, or belief that you think to be true and which restricts you in some way. This could be about anything like your interactions with other people or with the world and how it works.

Limiting beliefs can have a number of adverse effects on you.

One such limiting belief was highlighted in a study known as the Terman Study of the Gifted. It is considered to be the oldest and the longest-running study in the field of psychology.

An IQ test was given to 250,000 California school children and the top 120 among them were identified. These were kids with an IQ of 140 plus. A person with such an IQ is considered to be a genius, or, should I say that we believe that such a person will turn out to be a genius and will do something extraordinary in life, because this has been the perception throughout the years that high IQ is directly related to one's success.

Coming back to the study, these 120 students were tracked for the rest of their lives to figure out what happened to them.

So invested were they in the notion that IQ is the single most determinant factor of life success that the researcher believed those who had been identified in this study will turn out to be people who would excel at whatever they put their hands on. They may end up running top organizations or will probably be top politicians or top intellectuals. So, they were followed for a course of 20 to 30 years.

But what the researchers found out after following their subjects for so many years was that what they believed was not true at all.

It was only the top 15 percent that occupied positions of real prominence in society and the other big group in the middle had average lives. These kids were now adults with genius level IQ and there was this chunk at the bottom who turned out to be failures and whose lives, to say the least, were disappointing.

What this study tells us is that heavily ingrained beliefs can be wrong if one dives deep into it and looks for rationality.

Such a belief and many other that we have tattooed on our brains could keep us away from making good choices, grabbing new opportunities, or reaching our true potential. Ultimately, limiting beliefs can keep one stuck in a harmful state of mind and deter that person from living the life they truly desire.

In a scene from the movie V for Vendetta, Natalia Portman's character, Evey, realizes that she had the ability to leave the prison all along and that she was only being kept in her cell by her expectations which her brain was creating for her based on the inputs that she was getting, but she never thought to test it. And when she did, she realized that she was being limited only by her own expectations.

In a study performed at Dartmouth College, an ugly scar with the help of make-up was placed on the faces of a few participants. They were then sent into a room for a conversation and were asked to report how people responded to their scars. But here's the twist — right before they left, the experimenter said, "Hold on a minute. We just want to touch up your scars."

But instead of touching up, they removed the scars entirely.

So, the participants went into the conversation thinking that they still had the scars when, in fact, they were looking completely normal. Despite this, they came back and reported how awkward their conversation was, and how people avoided looking at their scars. They were not making eye contact and were tense and uncomfortable with their conversation. Their belief regarding their scars led them to believe the things that weren't even there. What could have been a perfectly normal conversation became an awkward one, because their belief created a reality which wasn't real at all.

How to Identify Your Limiting Beliefs?

So, how do you identify limiting beliefs? There are a number of ways by which you can do so, and most require some amount of personal reflection.

Seeing as they may not be simply recognizable, here are a couple of methods you could try to bring them to the surface.

1. Identify and Write Down Your Beliefs

To recognize the beliefs that are limiting you, start by writing down your general beliefs. Write down beliefs about anything you feel strongly about and which affect your daily life. Group them into different categories like family, relationships, or health. Once you've done this, pick which ones are helping you grow and which could be limiting you.

2. Evaluate Your Behavior

Another approach you can take to identifying limiting beliefs is to assess your behavior. Think about scenarios where you've acted in undesirable or negative ways and figure out why you did so. If you look closely at your irrational behaviors, you might discover that the underlying cause of them is limiting beliefs. For instance, if you find it difficult to speak your mind when someone has offended you, you may possess the limiting belief that conflict is bad. This, in turn, could keep you from having truly intimate relationships as you're unable to speak your mind and have healthy clashes. I experienced something similar when I joined theatre. I was the guy who would speak the least and just listen to others. There were people who would debate on topics and often would go at length to prove their points. There were conflicts over the topics which were discussed, but I would sit quietly, especially at the beginning, as I was a bit scared of conflicts and that too with people who were more learned than me. But with time, experience, and a bit of courage, I started participating and learned a great deal out of that experience.

3. Write Down Areas Where You Feel Tested

If you've noticed that you have recurring challenges in certain areas of your life, this could be indicative of limiting beliefs. Perhaps you can't seem to land a well-paid job, or you never have luck when it comes to love. These challenges may simply be the byproduct of wrong beliefs that your brain has accepted as truths. As you go through each challenge, write them down. Also make a note of which of your beliefs pertain to that particular challenge.

CHAPTER VII

COMMUNICATION IS CONNECTING

"Connection is why we're here: it is what gives purpose and meaning to our lives"
- Brene Brown

MAKE CONNECTIONS LIKE POETS OF ICELAND

Iceland is a country of majestic landscapes and sheep speckled countryside. There are a number of theories out there about why Iceland is such of blossoming land of poetry. The reason that there are more poets per capita in Iceland than in any other country of the world is that reciting the sagas have become a way for the Icelanders to keep their consciousness preserved in an environment which is exceedingly hostile to human existence.

Iceland has a long history of poetry and when you look at their environment you will see that for them poetic inspiration isn't that hard to come by.

When the Nordic settlers first arrived in Iceland, it seems they wrote the famous Poetic Edda — a series of poems telling the tales of Old Norse Gods like Thor and Loki. The love of poetry is still prevalent there and, through the ages, Iceland has had many magnificent poets.

Isolated in freezing nights, they used to enchant their poems huddled around fires in precarious huts. If the Icelanders had spent all those nights in silence listening to the mocking wind, their minds would have soon filled with dread and despair. Utilitarian ideologies in the past two centuries or so have convinced us that the main purpose of talking is to convey useful information.

Thus, we value terse (brief and to the point, effectively cut short) communication which reduces anything else to be a frivolous waste of time. We only aim at what we value. We pay attention to selective things we can get out of communication, and which can be of value to us.

There is a concept that explains it better. It was demonstrated by the cognitive psychologist, Daniel Simmons. Simmons' best work includes change blindness and inattentional blindness. His research also includes

122

visual cognition, perception, memory, attention, and awareness.

In the demonstration, Simmons showed a video of two teams of three people. One team was wearing white shirts and the other team was in black shirts.

Each team had its own ball, which they bounced and passed on to their team members, as they moved around in a small space where this game was filmed. Daniel showed this video to his participants. He asked each one of them to count the number of times the white shirts team members threw the ball back and forth to one another and report the number of passes they made. Most of them answered "15" which was indeed the correct answer. The participants felt pretty good about answering it correctly and thought that they had passed the test.

But then Dr. Simmons asked, "Did you see the gorilla?"

The participants were amazed at the question and felt that it was a joke.

So, he said, "Watch the video again. But this time, don't count."

Surely enough, a minute into the video, a man dressed in a gorilla suit walks right into the middle of the game for a few long seconds, stops, and then beats his chest exactly like how gorillas do everywhere.

He was there in the video, right in the middle of it, and starkly conspicuous, but still one out of every two of his participants missed it the first time they saw the video.

There was another experiment done by Dr. Simmons.

In that, he showed his participants a video of someone being served at a counter. The server dips behind the counter for a moment to get something and then comes back up. Most of his participants were unable to detect anything, but it was a different person who had stood up in the original server's place.

Similarly, our urge to only pick out the things we value may result in us missing out on something important or vital.

This is a pity as the fundamental function of conversation is not to get things accomplished but to improve the quality of the experience.

BREAKING THE ICE

People are like an open book because while some people are easy to understand, others remain a mystery. Let's say you are out for dinner with your friends and get joined by a friend of a friend whom you don't know. Now, if you are someone who is humorous and jokes come to you naturally, then building a rapport with that person won't be much of a task. But if you are like me, whose jokes fall flat most of the time, then it may be difficult for you to break the ice. One of the solutions for that would be to talk about something they're interested in or talk about what they are wearing or what their hobbies are, so on and so forth.

For instance, let me share with you an example of a friend

He had a business meeting with one of his clients. The person came across as a tough, no bullshit, only to the point guy, and as a result of it my friend was having a difficult time in trying to build a rapport with him. So, he was curious to figure out a way to overcome this. He noticed that the client would wear a fancy looking silver chain with beads on it during every meeting, and one day he asked him about it. A big beam lit up the man's face and he went on and on telling him how this chain was given to him by his mother and how he had been wearing it since he was in college, and how he believed that it brought him luck.

This story gave my friend a whole new impression of this man's love for his mother his appreciation of her support. It also told him that little things were really important to this man. One innocent question opened up a whole world of someone else's reality to him. I can't emphasize enough how important it is to ask questions when you communicate.

We have the tendency to not ask questions and jump to conclusions even before the other person has completed his or her statement. We don't even realize that most of the time we are so eager to jump to a conclusion without getting the entire message that it impacts the outcome of the very problem for which the communication was started at the first place.

The same thing happened with Ernesto Sirolli, when he went to Africa for one of his projects

Ernesto Sirolli is an Italian author and public speaker with expertise in the field of local economics. He is the author of books, Ripples from Zambezi and How to Start A Business and Ignite Your Life. He gained international attention in 2012 with his TEDx talk 'shut up and listen'.

The presentation received over 3 million views and was included in TED's founder book; *Ted Talk; The Official Guide to Public Speaking.*

In his talk at Ted, he spoke about a project that he had set up in Africa, which failed.

During that time, he was working in an Italian NGO.

In one of his projects, they decided to teach the Zambian people how to grow tomatoes. However, the locals had no interest in it. So, they paid them to come and work along instead of asking them, 'How come they are not growing anything?'

They focused on doing it themselves. Everything grew incredibly well.

He mentioned that the tomatoes they grew in Zambia were much bigger than the tomatoes found in Italy, his home country. Proud of their achievement, they started telling the Zambian people that growing tomatoes is easy and that they could do it too. They thought, at least for some time, that they had achieved success with their project. But the problem was far from over; and what happened one night was quite astonishing. Around two hundred hippos came out of the river during the night and ate everything, destroying the field completely.

Ernesto and his team were shocked. The Zambian people, on the other hand, were familiar with such events and they told Ernesto and his team that this was the reason for which they refused to grow the tomatoes.

Ernesto asked them why they didn't say this before, and they replied:

"Because you never asked!'

Questioning is a uniquely powerful tool for unlocking value in communications. It branches learning and exchange of ideas, fuels innovations and performance improvement, and builds rapport and trust. And above all, it can mitigate risk. Sometimes the best way to have a constructive conversation is to give a little less advice and ask a few more questions.

To be mindful of communication essentially means to listen and think before speaking, to be mindful of what you say, and to communicate with kindness and awareness. You can see from the above example how asking questions, in the right way, is a form of mindful communication. You also need to stop and listen to the answers rather than jumping in to express your own thoughts upon them.

For starters, asking questions provides you with feedback, as the answers you receive will offer insight into the situation at hand. The answers will also reassure you of the fact that you're being helpful, even if you don't feel like you are doing much by simply asking questions.

INFERIORITY/SUPERIORITY

Connections are hindered when we believe in the concept of superior and inferior. An inferiority complex is "a lack of self-esteem."

Some people with inferiority complexes cope with it by overcompensating in other directions — by being an overachiever, by socially removing oneself from others, by developing a superficial superiority complex, or a combination of all of these.

A superiority complex can be termed as a coping mechanism to deal with an inferiority complex, which means that someone with a superiority complex will assert their superiority despite of their own feelings of inferiority.

Just to clarify, everyone with a superiority complex has an inferiority complex, but not everyone with an inferiority complex develops a superiority complex. A superiority complex is only one of many coping mechanisms.

And both are not very appropriate for the appetite when it comes to making connections with others. As soon as we drop the weight of these two from our self-standard, we experience a connection.

A superiority complex and an inferiority complex are both echoes of the way we feel about ourselves. In both cases, there is an inability to accurately see one's worth, skill level, or agreeableness in comparison to others.

Superiority complex refers to the feeling of superiority or 'being better' than others and having an exaggerated self-worth, whereas inferiority complex is the feeling of insignificance or 'being lesser' than others.

While the former is overly confident, the latter tend to doubt their capabilities. Moreover, someone dealing with a superiority complex may hide their feelings of low self-esteem and self-worth, while someone with an inferiority complex might hide their aspirations and goals.

Brian Wind clinical psychologist, and chief clinical officer of Journey Pure, says the theory of individual psychology dictates that we all are working hard to improve our skills and achieve more to overcome inherent feelings of inferiority so that we can be successful in our own eyes. "Hence, a superiority complex can be a reaction to our failure to meet our own expectations. On the other hand, a person with inferiority complex may always be modest or downplay their achievements. They may actually have high aspirations for themselves but fear that they may not achieve them. So, they downplay what they have achieved to lower people's expectations of them," he explains.

Honestly for me, from the shoe polisher outside Metro to the CEO of a bank are both kind of people who are superior to me in certain aspects.

But neither of them can restore a smile to a scared face or do any number of other things as well as I can.

Shakespeare apparently talked with many people when writing his play, King Lear. He even spoke to people whom some might call stupid. He talked to the stupid doorkeepers, the stupid property men, with stupid apprentices, and had much pleasure in ascertaining from them their notion of *King Lear*.

The feeling of inferiority comes about for just one reason. We judge ourselves not against our own norm but against someone else's norm.

When we do this, we always, without exception, come out as second best. But because we think, believe, and assume that we should measure up to some other person's norm, we feel miserable and second-rate and eventually conclude that there is something wrong with us.

And it shows in our communication when we try to connect with others. We often under such feelings fail to communicate with conviction and downplay ourselves and our message.

We don't feel free to express ourselves which results in resentment and disappointment.

The truth is:

You are not 'inferior'

You are not 'superior'

You are simply 'you'

According to a report in science digest, a psychologist wanted to find out how feelings of inferiority affected the ability to solve problems.

He gave students a set of routine tests and then solemnly declared that a normal person could complete the test in about one fifth the time it would otherwise take. When the test would be in progression, a bell would ring which would signify that the average man's time is up.

Some of the brightest subjects became nervous and incompetent, thinking of themselves to be morons.

This is how such belief impacts our minds. God has created all sorts of people — tall and short, large and people, skinny and fat, black, brown and white — but has never indicated any preference for any one size, shape, or color. So, stop downplaying or undermining yourself.

HELL OR HEAVEN – HOW TOASTMASTER HELPED

A woman who had worked all her life for good causes had a strange wish. She asked God, "Before I die, let me visit both Hell and Heaven." God granted her the wish and she was taken to Hell first.

To her surprise, she found that it was a vast, beautiful, and elegant banquet hall. As far as the eyes could see, the tables were piled with delicious food and drink. Around the table sat a bunch of people – but they were miserable and starving

She asked "Why are they like that?"

The Messenger replied, "Look at their spoons."

She looked and saw that the handles were so long that those people couldn't use the spoon to put food in their mouth.

This is Hell!

Then she was taken to Heaven.

To her amazement, she found herself in an identical place, a vast banquet hall. Again, with tables piled with delicious food and drink. And again, there were people sitting around the tables. But this time, they were happy, joyful, and well-nourished.

"But how can they eat?" She asked.

"In heaven," The Messenger replied, "They feed each other."

This is what toastmaster did to me. Toastmaster is a platform where you can make your communication skills shine from scratch. There are more than 15,800 clubs in 149 countries; and you will find many in India. I would recommend you to join a club near you if you want to improve your public speaking skills, leadership skills, or gaining an advantage at your workplace or your social circle.

Why I wanted to join Toastmasters?

Because I lacked the confidence to come up on stage and speak. If I did speak, I lacked content. I lacked social skills.

What did I learn at Toastmasters?

It is the best platform that provides a friendly environment to break the ice on stage, interact with strangers, and learn in moments of fun.

Also, table topics, playing roles improve your impromptu speaking skills. Prepared speeches, the spirit of TI, makes you more disciplined as you are focused on addressing a speech in a limited amount of time without affecting the core idea of the speech, so you start preparing, structuring, brainstorming for it right from the start with a good plan.

Apart from that, the mentor-mentee relationship is what I found to be the most productive part of Toastmasters. It is the only organization where people support, help, and guide each other without any returns! The same goes for speech evaluation too.

These are just to name a few among many others benefits of joining a Toastmasters club.

STAY AWAY FROM TOXICITY

When I was in school, I wasn't able to learn much or pay much attention to class because my brain was preoccupied with the need for friendship/social circle. People who have been bullied or had difficulty in maintaining companionship would understand what I'm saying better.

So why would someone sit in the classroom and bother to learn about Pythagoras theorem when he is afraid to walk home alone or, if he is afraid, what will happen when class gets and he has to think about the difficulty to connect with other classmates when the lunch bell rings? This inability to connect with another individual can honestly haunt you. We are all social animals and we love to be in groups, and surrounded by people. Children want it more than adults.

You may have great skills and great qualifications, but if you are put in a toxic environment, it will be very difficult for you to use those skills effectively.

The toxic environment here is the need for being in a group that doesn't accept you as you are. You should not long to fit in but to belong in a group. This becomes toxic for you as you try to do things to please others.

It is needed for survival. One does things just to be included in a social circle and most of the time these things that we do are not right in our senses or is against our better judgement. But we still do it, because it is about survival and the need to be socially accepted, as this is what our conditioning has done to us. A message has been indirectly spread across that staying in a herd is the safest thing to do, be it in personal or professional life.

There is no connection when the mind works according to this criterion.

You will only just survive with such beliefs and thriving in any field will be a distant dream for you if you're hooked on to this socio norm.

LET'S GET OUT OF THIS DITCH TOGETHER

A guy falls into a hole, and the sides of the hole are so high that he can't get out.

Soon, a doctor walks out. The guy screams to the doctor for help.

"Please get me out of here, I am stuck!"

The doctor writes a prescription, throws it down, and walks away.

The Guy is still stuck in the hole. He waits, and then a priest walks by. He shouts, ''Please help me get out of here!''

The priest prays for him and walks away. The guy is still stuck in the hole.

He waits...

A friend walks out.

"Shreya! Shreya!" He yells, "Help me out. I am stuck in a hole."

She says to him, "Don't worry, I know exactly what needs to be done." She jumps into the hole herself and now they are both stuck. He says, what you have done! Now we are both stuck inside this hole."

She looks at him, smiles, and says, "I have been down here before and I know the way out."

The connections we make with people will help us no matter what hole we are stuck in. We need medication, we need religious strength; they are important, yes, but they are nothing without strong relationships with people.

People watch a reality show on television where two equally talented singers sing the same song. One of them gives the audience goosebumps while the other leaves everybody cold. Why is that?

Two professors at a university teach the same class at the same time using the same prescribed syllabus and required textbook. Students stand in line at registrations to get into the first teachers' class while the other teacher's class starts below capacity and dwindle further to just a few students. Why?

Two managers work together running a restaurant. All twenty employees work regularly for each of them. When the first manager needs extra help and asks people to work late, they do so willingly. But when the other manager makes the same appeal the following week, all the employees make excuses for why they can't stay. What's the reason for this difference?

Two parents raise a child together in the same household, applying the same rules. One parent gets cheerful obedience while the other gets resistance. Why?

Shouldn't the words of the song arouse the same response from both singers?

Shouldn't the same course be equally interesting to students?

Shouldn't both managers expect to be given the same obedience?

Shouldn't the parents in the same household encourage the same reaction?

You probably know the answer is no. But why?

Because people respond to others not merely because of the words that are used but on the connection they make with that person. When people try to communicate with others, many believe that the message is all that matters.

But the reality is that communication goes way beyond words.

In an important study, UCLA psychology professor emeritus, Albert Mehrabian, discovered that face-to-face communication can be broken down into three components: words, tone of voice, and body language.

What may come as surprise is that in some situations, such as verbal and non-verbal, messages aren't consistent. What people see us doing and the tone we use can far outweigh any words we say while trying to communicate.

In situations where feelings and attitude are being communicated:

- What we say accounts for only 7 percent of what is believed.
- The way we say it accounts for 38 percent.
- What others see account for 55 percent.

Amazingly, more than 90 percent of the impression we often transport has nothing to do with what we actually say.

So, if you believe communication is all about words, you're totally missing the beat, and you will always have a hard time connecting with others.

TAKE A COMPLIMENT

In previous chapters we have talked about how complimenting others can add life to a dying conversation.

Usually, the practice should be more towards giving a compliment but let's now talk about taking a compliment. This is not to undermine the importance of the primary one, for both are equally important.

So, how do you feel when someone pays you a compliment? For instance, when someone says you look good or you have accomplished something inspiring, do you downplay it? For many people, compliments feel both pleasant and a little awkward, and they don't quite know how to handle them. Many of us either turn shy or modestly rub off the compliment by saying something like, "Oh, it's nothing..."

Unfortunately, doing this sends a message to your admirer that they were mistaken in complimenting you. They will probably feel rather foolish, and there's even a chance that they will associate this experience of feeling foolish with you. If you do this often enough, pretty soon they'll stop trying. But if, on the other hand, you make them feel good for complimenting you, they'll enjoy feeling good about themselves, and so will want to do it again.

The next time you're given a compliment, the following steps will help you skillfully handle the moment:

1. Stop.

2. Absorb the compliment. Enjoy it, if you can.

3. Let that second of fascination show on your face. Show the person that they've had an influence on you.

4. Thank them. Saying "Thank you very much" is enough, but you can take it a step further by thanking them for their thoughtfulness or telling them that they've made your day with their appreciation.

I remember back in the day when I used to attend training at my workplace and the trainers we had used to follow this approach. But they did it with enthusiasm and not just for the sake of it, or because it was the right thing to do. They would stop and absorb it first and then go on to thank the other person by adding lines such as, "You have made my day" or "That is so wonderful of you to think of me in this way." They always went a step ahead and were amazing at their craft. This, of course, comes with practice. There's bound to be hesitation initially, but as you repeat it on every such occasion, it'll slowly get ingrained in you and sooner rather than later will come naturally to you.

As Dale Carnegie said, "You can make more friends in two months by becoming truly interested in other people than you can in two years by trying to get other people interested in you."

One great trick is to imagine that the person you're speaking with is the main star in a movie that you're watching right now.

This will help you find them more interesting, and there's even a chance that you'll actually make them feel like a movie star. Charismatic people are masters at using positive associations, whether consciously or subconsciously, and you'll often hear people rave about how "special" and "wonderful" these charismatics made them feel.

BUILDING RAPPORT THROUGH MIRRORING

What is mirroring?

Mirroring is the behavior in which one person unconsciously imitates the gesture, speech pattern, or attitude of another.

Mirroring often occurs in social situations, particularly in the company of close friends or family. The concept often affects another individuals' notions about the one who is exhibiting mirroring behaviors, which can lead to an individual building rapport with others.

It is the subconscious replication of another person's nonverbal signals.

This concept takes place in everyday interactions and often goes unnoticed by both the person enacting the mirroring behaviors as well as the one who is being mirrored. Mirroring establishes rapport with the individual who is being mirrored, as the similarities in nonverbal gestures allow the individual to feel more connected with the person exhibiting the mirrored behavior.

Have you ever noticed that people who have been married for many years often end up looking like each other?

It's actually a well-documented fact that as we spend more and more time together, we adapt to each other's body language. This includes our facial expressions, which end up shaping our faces in similar ways by repeatedly using the same facial muscles. If both you and your partner are sad most of the time then you will develop a sad face. If both of you are happy most of the time then your face will give an impression of a happy person.

This tendency to mimic the body language of others is technically called limbic resonance, and it's infused into the human brain. Limbic resonance is made imaginable and further possible because of a certain class of neurons called oscillators which coordinate people physically by regulating how and when their bodies move together.

Daniel Goleman details in the Harvard Business Review what happens when two accomplished cellists play together. Not only do they hit their notes in unison but, thanks to oscillators, their right brain hemispheres are more closely coordinated with each other's than they are to the left hemispheres of their own brains! Imitating someone's body language is an easy way to create trust and rapport. This technique, which is often called mirroring or mimicking, is the mindful application of something that many people do instinctively.

When you consciously mirror someone's body language, you trigger deep instincts of trust and fondness. For this reason, it can be a great aid when you need people to open up to you.

During your next few conversations, try to mirror the other person's overall posture — the way they hold their head, how they place their feet. If they move their left hand, move your right hand. Aim also to adapt your voice to theirs in speed, pitch, and intonation.

Because people focus primarily on themselves while interacting, they usually won't notice that you're mirroring them unless you are exceedingly clear about it. However, here are some ways to increase subtlety:

• Be choosy: Do only what feels normal to you. For instance, some gestures are gender-specific.

• Use variations in fullness: If they make a large gesture, you could make a smaller one.

• Use time: Let a few seconds pass before you move into a mirrored position.

Mirroring someone's body language is often sufficient to achieve rapport and sometimes adequate to bring them around to your point of view. Mirroring is also one of the few methods that can help overcome a bad first impression. It's extremely effective. When we mirror, as the name suggests, we play the role of a real mirror by physically describing how they look or act. Although we may not understand somebody's stories or facts, we can see their actions and reflect them back to that person. Mirroring is most helpful when another person's tone of voice or gestures (hints about the emotions behind them) are varying with his or her words.

For example: "Don't worry. I'm fine." (But the person in question is saying this with a look and tone that suggests he is actually quite upset. He's scowling, looking around, and sort of kicking at the ground.)

"Really? From the way you're saying that, it doesn't sound like you are."

We point out to them that while they may be saying one thing, their tone of voice or body posture is indicating something else. In doing so, by staying with the detected actions, we show both respect and concern for that person.

When reflecting back on your observations, take care to manage your tone of voice and delivery. It is not the fact that we are acknowledging someone's emotions that creates safety, but when our tone of voice says we're okay with it.

So, as we describe what we see, we have to do so with tranquilly. If we act upset or as though we're not going to like what they'll say, we won't build safety. We will reinforce and validate their doubts that they need to remain silent.

Examples of mirroring include:

"You say you're fine, but by the tone of your voice, you seem distressed."

"You seem annoyed at me."

"You look anxious about confronting him. Are you sure you're ready to do it?"

As the two individuals in this situation display similar nonverbal gestures, they may believe that they share similar attitudes and ideas as well.

Rapport is an important part of social life, as creating rapport with a person is generally the first step to becoming friends or acquaintances with them.

It can help you build relationships with friends, clients, and strangers

Tom Hoobyar, in his book about NLP, mentions an activity that he was a part of. He walked into a room and saw pairs of chairs that had been placed back-to-back. He sat on one chair and the other person sat on the chair behind him.

With the trainer and another person standing there as observers.

The trainer told them to have a discussion about anything and to agree with each other. The observer was told to just watch and notice the process. So, they began the conversation with things like — what a nice day it is, how interesting the training is, and so on. This went on for a while. Then the instructor stopped them and asked them to have another conversation but this time disagreeing with each other.

So, they started and Tom said, "Well, I think women have way too many rights in the society. It was a lot better when they were stuck in the bedroom. The woman on the receiving end hit back strongly at Tom and argued fiercely with his statement and point of view. This too went on for a while.

Then the trainer interrupted and stopped them again.

He then told them to turn their chairs towards each other, and asked the observer to share what he noticed.

The observer said when the partners were having the conversation (agreeable one), no matter how they were sitting, when the exercise began their posture actually changed and mirrored the person whose back was at them.

- Heads tilted in the same way
- Gestures where synchronized
- Legs crossed the same way

The trainer then asked what happened when the partners were engaged in a conversation where they disagreed.

The observer said:

- They went completely out of sync with each other
- Body positions were closed and different from each other
- Their gestures and facial expression were out of tune with each other

Outcome – mirroring is not complicated and you don't have to remember too many things. To have a rapport and connection with another person, just being curious about their emotional state is enough.

CONNECTING WITH PEOPLE AT ALL LEVELS

CONNECTING PRINCIPLE: Connecting or interacting meaningfully with someone always requires energy. The larger the group, the more energy that's required to connect.

connecting one to one

Many people get lazy when it comes to connecting one-on-one. They take for granted that people will listen to them and they don't have to make much effort to make their point. But that's being unfair to others, especially the people who are closest to you, such as your friends and family. The next time you try to connect with someone one-on-one, gear up for it mentally and emotionally, just as you would for an audience. If you bring deliberate energy to the conversation, you make it much easier for people to connect with you. Speak enthusiastically and listen patiently.

connecting in a group

When you communicate with a group or in a meeting, the energy in the room can vary radically. Sometimes the group itself will bring a lot of energy to the process and carry the day, while at other times as the leader or communicator, you will need to take lead and generate energy.

The next time you communicate in a group, don't allow yourself to become complacent. Bring energy to the process and then continue bringing it—even if the energy in the room is good. Just don't stop.

The experience will be better for everyone if you remain intentionally active. In addition, you will gain people's admiration if you take responsibility for the energy level. When I used to attend 8-hour long session and trainers would feel that people are dozing off, they would immediately ask all the people in the room to stand up and engage in some sort of activity. This trick or approach would invariably charge the participants back to an active state. This is just one of the examples, or hacks, that can be implemented when you are facilitating a group.

When I take sessions, the few guidelines which I keep in mind are worth looking into:

• Before the session begins, I go to each person and introduce myself.

• I ask each individual a question to learn something exclusive about him or her.

• At the start of the session I give them ownership of the meeting. They ask me questions, and I do my best to answer them.

I ask them about their expectations from the session which I'm going to commence.

Don't Make Statements Disguised as Questions

Anyone who has ever in a car as a kid has expressed the irritable words — "Are we there yet?" You know you're not there yet, and your parents know you know, and so they respond in a tone as irritable as yours.

What you really meant was, "I'm feeling agitated" or "I wish we were there" or "This is a stretched trip for me." Any of these would likely have prompted a more productive response from your parents.

This exemplifies an important rule about inquiry: If you don't have a question, don't ask one.

Never camouflage an assertion as a question. Doing so creates misunderstanding and bitterness because such questions are certainly perceived as mocking and sometimes even mean spirited.

Consider some examples of assertions masked as questions: "Are you going to leave the refrigerator door open like that?" (Instead of "Please close the refrigerator door" or "I feel angry when you leave the refrigerator door open.")

"Is it so difficult for you to focus on me just once?" (Instead of "I feel unnoticed" or "I'd like you to pay more attention to me.")

"Do you have to drive so fast?" (Instead of "I'm feeling nervous") or I feel uncomfortable when you drive so fast."

Notice that these examples of enveloped assertions are either about feelings or requests.

This should hardly be surprising, because sharing our feelings and making requests are two things that many of us have trouble doing directly. They can make us feel vulnerable or even embarrassed. However, turning what we have to say into an attack — a sarcastic question — can feel harmless and easier to do. But this safety is an illusion, and we lose more than we gain from it.

Saying "I'd like you to pay more attention to me" is more likely to produce a conversation (and a satisfying outcome) than "Is it impossible for you to focus on me just once?"

Don't Use Questions to Cross-Examine

A second error that gets us into trouble is using questions to make holes in the other person's argument. For example:

"You appear to think that this is my fault. But surely, you'd agree that you made more errors than I did, wouldn't you?"

"If it's true that you did everything you could have done to make the sale, how do you explain the fact that Sagar was able to make the sale right after you gave up?"

These questions are incorrect from the start. They originate from a purpose of trying to coax the other person into admitting that you are right and they are wrong, instead of trying to learn.

These things should always be kept in mind when having a conversation with a third party.

YOU ARE SAFE WITH ME

When meeting a stranger for the first time, making them feel safe/comfortable in your company is key to creating a connection.

To achieve this, one must control their own incongruence, anxiety, or feeling of self-doubt. That's not about other people's job, that's an inside job for some of us who have an issue of being shy. This shyness is going to set off an alert in other people's minds because it is going to make them very uncomfortable.

Basically, it is communicated to the other person that we are so self-involved and preoccupied within ourselves that we're not really paying attention to them or what they're saying. We are nervous, our eyes are darting around, and we are fidgeting, making uncomfortable facial expressions. These behaviors don't bring comfort to another person.

To make someone else comfortable, we first have to be comfortable within ourselves. For those who view communication as a war of arguments, it's the voices in their own heads that are crushing them.

When such people are not talking, they are thinking about what they'll say next. The solution to this is to focus on another person and make them feel safe. The voices in the head will automatically begin to quiet down. An amount of internal work must be done before we can put someone at ease when interacting with us. There are a few things that can help you make another person comfortable and one of them, perhaps the most basic yet important one, is being polite.

Good communication happens if you are polite and soft spoken.

Loud and impolite conversations never harvest the right results but talking with courteousness and maintaining a good body language can help you connect with anyone. One can learn a lot from people working as cabin crew when it comes to talking with strangers the right way. Being a flight attendant means that you need to interact with passengers who usually are all strangers. However, due to the nature of their job, it's imperative for them to make a positive impression on passengers by having the right social and communication skills. In their training, they are taught to use the right tone to convey what they are saying to their passengers so that it leaves a good impression upon them. Even if a passenger is rude, their tone is supposed to be calm and friendly. They are also trained about making eye contact when talking to passengers and are educated about the importance of eye contact while interacting. It should be such that you can show that you are listening and are interested in what others are saying, but not keep it for too long because it may seem like you are staring at the other person.

Or, take for example the case of better.com and how their communication about laying off the staff had taken the internet by storm, where many CEOs of different companies condemned the way, the message was communicated.

Vishal Garg, Chief Executive Officer of Better.com, even apologized for the manner in which he handled the mass layoff at the US-based online mortgage firm.

Garg apologized for the way he (mis)handled the layoff, by writing: *"I failed to show the appropriate amount of respect and appreciation for the individuals who were affected and for their contributions to Better. I own the decision to do the layoffs, but in communicating it I blundered the execution. In doing so, I embarrassed you."*

Garg had received severe flak after a video of him firing 900 people, nearly 9% of the company's workforce, via a Zoom call that went viral on social media. Memes about the video even landed on the TikTok app as people all over the world trashed Garg's actions.

Garg's repute as a not-so-nice leader goes back to a time when forbes had revealed the contents of an email from Garg to his employees: "HELLO — WAKE UP BETTER TEAM. You are TOO DAMN SLOW. You are a bunch of DUMB DOLPHINS and...DUMB DOLPHINS get caught in nets or eaten by sharks. SO STOP IT. STOP IT. STOP IT RIGHT NOW. YOU ARE EMBARRASSING ME."

This gives out a stark message that one should not expect a person to be good at communication just because they have the credential of being toppers of B-schools or prestigious universities around the globe.

Interviewers and recruiters often look for candidates coming out of top B-schools. Even if they are looking for a candidate with more than ten years of experience, then also such academic history is taken into consideration and relied upon heavily in favor of the candidate who has passed out from a top B-school, and not the other candidate who has graduated from an average college. Despite the fact that this ten-year gap between college and the present day might have made the guy who passed from an average college more skilled than the one who has passed out of a top B-school. The latter might just be enjoying the perks of making a one-time effort of getting selected to a prestigious university with a high IQ and lacking in other areas which matter more than IQ, and which the former might be possessing or might have learned along his journey.

One should not assume that such a person will naturally be gifted with the requisite communication skills to handle tough situations.

It is a skill like any other skill and may not be naturally infused in a person with a high IQ and with glorious academic credentials. Regardless of one's academic qualification, a person has to practice the art of communication if they want to lead effectively in life, both professionally and personally.

In simple words, it's important to connect with people in a way that feels like they are a part of ourselves living, maybe a variation or extension of us leading a different life, and this includes the way we communicate with people around us.

Everything in life is about community and we can all make it better by communicating better.

Author's Note

Thank you to each and everyone who has picked up this book and decided to put their precious time into reading it.

I hope you would benefit from this book in some way or the other. Please share your experience with me.

You can connect with me on my email – 600.varun@gmail.com Or Instagram - Varunspeakinghere